NO ORDINARY JOURNEY

JOHN RAE, ARCTIC EXPLORER 1813-1893

1862   W. Armstrong

NO ORDINARY JOURNEY

JOHN RAE·ARCTIC EXPLORER 1813-1893

Ian Bunyan, Jenni Calder, Dale Idiens, Bryce Wilson

NATIONAL MUSEUMS OF SCOTLAND
Edinburgh

McGill-Queen's University Press
Montreal & Kingston • London • Buffalo

Published by the National Museums of Scotland,
Chambers Street, Edinburgh EH1 1JF

ISBN 0 948636 38 6 (paper)
ISBN 0 948636 39 4 (cloth)

Published simultaneously in Canada by
McGill-Queen's University Press

ISBN 0 7735 1107 5 (paper)
ISBN 0 7735 1106 7 (cloth)

Legal deposit first quarter 1993
Bibliothèque Nationale du Québec

Designed and produced by the Publications Office
of the National Museums of Scotland
Additional photography by
National Museums of Scotland Photographic Services

Printed by Craftprint (Singapore) Ltd

British Library Cataloguing in Publication Data

A catalogue record for this book is available from the British Library.

Canadian Cataloguing in Publishing Data

1. Rae, John, 1813-1893.
2. Arctic regions - Discovery and exploration - British.
3. Northwest, Canadian - Discovery and exploration - British.

I   Idiens, Dale   II Wilson, Bryce

FC3961.1.R33N6 1993   917.1904´1´092

F1060.8.N6 1993   C92-090651-6

*We of the Hudson's Bay Company
thought very little of our Arctic
work. For my own part at least
I thought no more of it than any
ordinary journey.*

John Rae
Letter to R H Major,
June 1875

Frontispiece: John Rae in the dress of a Cree Indian. Watercolour by William Armstrong, 1862.

Page v: Looking north through Robeson Channel. Detail from a watercolour by Thomas Mitchell, 1875.

Page viii: Map showing the Arctic travels of John Rae.

Page x: Expedition boat on Hawk Rapids, Back River, 1834. Detail from a drawing by George Back.

Page xi: Stone cairn, 'Last resting place of 1 or more of Franklin's men.' Detail from the notebook of W Klutschak, 1879.

CONTENTS

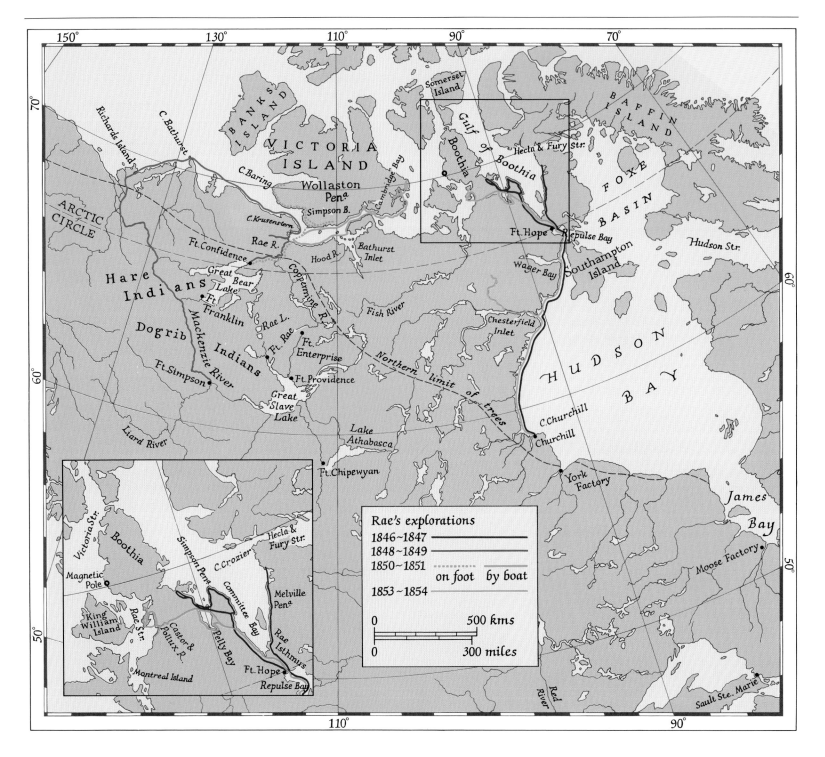

150°   130°   110°   90°   70°

70°

BANKS ISLAND

Richards Island
C.Bathurst
VICTORIA ISLAND
C.Baring
Wollaston Penᵃ
Cambridge Bay
Simpson B.
C.Krusenstern
Somerset Island
Gulf of Boothia
Boothia
BAFFIN ISLAND
Hecla & Fury Str.
FOXE BASIN

ARCTIC CIRCLE
Rae R.
Ft.Confidence
Hood R.
Coppermine R.
Bathurst Inlet
Ft.Hope   Repulse Bay
Hudson Str.

60°

Hare Indians
Great Bear Lake
Ft Franklin
Rae L.
Ft. Rae
Ft. Enterprise
Ft.Providence
Fish River
Northern limit of trees
Wager Bay
Southampton Island
HUDSON BAY
Chesterfield Inlet

Dogrib Indians
Mackenzie River
Ft.Simpson
Great Slave Lake

Liard River
Lake Athabasca
C.Churchill
Churchill

Ft.Chipewyan
York Factory

James Bay
Moose Factory

50°

INSET:
VictoriaStr.
Boothia
Magnetic Pole
King William Island
Rae Str.
Castor & Pollux R.
Montreal Island
Simpson Penᵃ
C.Crozier
C.Crozier
Committee Bay
Pelly Bay
Rae Isthmus
Ft.Hope
Repulse Bay
Hecla & Fury Str.
Melville Penᵃ

Rae's explorations
1846~1847
1848~1849
1850~1851   on foot   by boat
1853~1854

0 ————————— 500 kms

0 ————————— 300 miles

Red River
Sault Ste. Marie

110°   90°

VIII

PREFACE

John Rae gave over thirty years of his life to exploring, investigating and documenting the northern part of the American continent. He was a remarkable man, committed, independent and idiosyncratic, who contributed in many important ways to our understanding of the geography, climate, natural history and ethnography of one of the world's last frontier territories. The map of Canada pays tribute to his work, in the many geographical features that bear his name. But beyond that there has been little recognition of the importance and diversity of his achievement.

He was born, in 1813, and raised in Orkney, a rugged training ground for a challenging life. The skills he began to learn as a boy proved essential to his success as an Arctic explorer. Equally important was his sympathetic understanding of the environment and the people - Indians, Inuit, *voyageurs*, transplanted Scots and Orcadians - who inhabited it.

Rae died in London in 1893 and was buried in the kirkyard of St Magnus Cathedral in Kirkwall, Orkney. Material collected by Rae and items of equipment used by him on his Arctic journeys went to the National Museums of Scotland, to the British Museum and to Orkney. One hundred years after his death an exhibition, arranged by the National Museums of Scotland and the Orkney Museums Service, celebrates the life and achievements of this exceptional man.

No Ordinary Journey was planned and published in association with the exhibition on show in Edinburgh, Orkney and Canada. Its purpose is to highlight aspects of Rae's life and travels, against the background of his Orkney origins and the absorbing story of Arctic exploration. Up till now the story has been dominated by figures such as Sir John Ross, Sir James Clark Ross and, most of all, Sir John Franklin. The contribution

X

of Dr John Rae and the native Canadians he learned from was not appropriately acknowledged in his lifetime, and has never been given due weight by Arctic historians. One hundred years after his death, this publication is a contribution to the process of putting the record straight.

Mark Jones,

Director,
National Museums of Scotland

CHILDHOOD IN ORKNEY

Bryce Wilson

The Orkney Islands lie further north than Fort Churchill, outpost of the fur trade on the frozen shore of Canada's Hudson Bay. For almost two centuries these islands supplied many of the workers who manned the Hudson's Bay Company. Among them was one of the Company's most distinguished servants, Dr John Rae.

The London-based company began trading under a royal charter of 1670, with the monopoly of a vast fur-bearing area, Rupert's Land, around the Bay. Each year its supply ships crossed the Atlantic in early summer, loaded with trade-goods, returning in the autumn with a rich bounty of beaver and fox. When wars with France rendered the English Channel unsafe for shipping, Atlantic-bound vessels followed a safer route around the north of Scotland. In the fine natural harbour of Stromness in Orkney, they stocked up with fresh water and provisions and awaited a fair wind.

In 1702 there is the first record of a ship's captain's instructions to recruit Orcadians for Company service. By the end of the eighteenth century Orcadians made up more than three-quarters of the Company's workforce, and recruitment at Stromness continued until the year 1891. Why the inhabitants of this scattering of small islands were so suited to service in the rigours of Rupert's Land, and were content to be so employed, can best be answered by examining their history and culture.

Several million years ago, fish swam where Orkney is now. Their bodies remain in the Old Red Sandstone which almost totally makes up the island group. Then the passage of a glacier formed the rounded hills and undulating plains, and laid the basis of fertile soil.

Hunters and gatherers lived there at the end of the last Ice Age, but throughout the islands are seen the remains of a later race of farmers

Opposite: Rough seas off Yesnaby, Orkney. *Charles Tait*

Winter in Stromness. *Gunni Moberg*

and fishermen. Their village of Skarabrae, engulfed by a sandstorm and perfectly preserved, reveals Stone Age domesticity in intimate detail: Maeshowe, predating the pyramids of Egypt, is one of the finest neolithic tombs in Europe.

Two thousand years ago, a deteriorating climate had reduced the islands' sparse tree cover to a layer of peat. Broch towers defended the remaining fertile soil. Then, enigmatic 'symbol stones' showed the presence of the Picts - 'the painted people' - whose culture permeated northern Scotland. Some 1200 years ago, silhouetted sails heralded the invading Norse, who settled, farmed the islands, and extended their influence as far as Dublin. Norse families held their lands in perpetuity. (Their names remain throughout the islands, and speech preserves the intonation of their tongue.)

When, in the late fifteenth century, Orkney was pawned to Scotland in lieu of a royal dowry, the influx of Scots led to the decline of the Norse families through the erosion of their land holdings. The last vestige of their independence was crushed when Norse law was repealed. By the late seventeenth century, when the ships of the Hudson's Bay Company began to call, many Orcadians had been reduced to poverty, as W P L Thomson records in his *History of Orkney* (1987):

> Small acreages, subsistence methods and large families made it essential to earn a living beyond the bounds of the farm, but the lure of fishing, whaling and service with the Hudson's Bay Company were not entirely to be measured in terms of money. It was a way of life that combined farming, travel, comradeship and adventure in much the same proportions as had once sent their forebears on their viking voyages.

The Orcadians were highly esteemed as general servants of the Hudson's Bay Company:

> There can be no doubt that the people from the Orkneys who are of Norse ancestry, and are quite distinct from the Celtic highlanders, by their patience and perseverance, quiet disposition and industrious habits and power of endurance were peculiarly suited for the hardships of such a wilderness life and for dealing with the Indian tribes in that 'canny' way which begets confidence...
>
> Professor Bryce, *Transactions of Manitoba Historical and Scientific Society*, 1883-4

The lairds of Orkney disapproved of this employment, which deprived them of a fruitful source of cheap labour. The merchants of Stromness, however, acted as employment agents for the Company. They also stocked the ships with fresh water and provisions, and each year supplied merchandise to workers around the Bay.

By the end of the eighteenth century the shoreline of the sheltered harbour of Stromness was lined with houses and stores and stone piers; the narrow winding street tempted voyagers with a throng of inns and ale-houses. The arrival of the Bay ships in June was the highlight of the summer, when a round of parties culminated in a ball on the principal ship. Over the decades, legendary Bay Company figures passed

Stromness, Orkney, in the early nineteenth century. Engraving by William Daniell.

Memorial to John Rae, St Magnus Cathedral, Kirkwall.
Charles Tait

through Stromness, such as Samuel Hearne (one of the Company's most adventurous explorers), William Tomison from South Ronaldsay (who became the Company's first 'Chief Inland'), and George Simpson (Governor in Chief of the Hudson Bay territories). Few of the islanders who embarked rose above the rank of tradesman or labourer - Tomison, who joined the Company in 1760, was an exception - but it was in Orkney, towards the end of the Napoleonic Wars, that John Rae was born.

By the 1870s, Dr John Rae could look back on an active and eventful life. He had almost completed the mapping - begun by others - of Canada's Arctic coastline, traversing thousands of miles on foot, and overwintering his men without starvation or illness. His achievement as the first to bring evidence of the fate of Sir John Franklin's expedition was a striking instance of his skill and determination. In his latter years he wrote widely on the natural history, geography and anthropology of the North. In many ways he was the epitome of the gentleman scholar and adventurer, and represents a Victorian ideal of spirited enterprise.

Nevertheless, in an age which lauded individual heroism and achievement in the service of the Empire, the death of Rae in London in 1893 caused no ripple of national sentiment and prompted no public eulogy. To this day, there is no marble plaque for him among the great in Westminster Abbey, and no bronze statue overlooks the rushing traffic of the capital city.

An examination of the values of Rae's contemporaries may reveal reasons for this neglect. Through an unwavering belief in progress, bolstered by advances in science and industry and Britain's dominant naval and military might, the Victorian Establishment had a blind faith in its own physical and moral superiority. As a fur-trader, Rae was thought to be inferior to Britain's official naval explorers, despite his invaluable experience of life in the Arctic. His reliance on native methods of survival was looked on as, in the words of V Stefansson in his book *Unsolved Mysteries of the Arctic* (1934), a 'vulgar subterfuge'. Honest and forthright comments on Arctic exploration made influential enemies, while the unpalatable evidence of the Franklin tragedy raised public indignation and wrath.

But Rae was also, perhaps, a victim of his own success. Because he avoided disaster, his career did not capture the public imagination, as did that of Franklin, which is still a source of fascination. Arctic historians now regard Rae as one of the great figures of Arctic exploration. His means of survival, fine qualities of leadership and exceptional health and strength, made him second to none in his understanding of the task and his ability to carry it through.

Within two years of Rae's death in 1893, a memorial figure was placed on his native island, in the red sandstone cathedral of St Magnus. The figure lies there still, resplendent in repose, under a mantle of buffalo hide. In the leafy kirkyard, a plain marble cross marks Rae's grave.

Rae became an explorer almost by chance, but his early life in Orkney can be seen as a preparation for the challenge of the Arctic. Today the landscape and topography of the islands are continuing reminders of this early life. Climbing the steeps of Scorradale, in the southern part of the Orkney mainland between Stromness and Kirkwall, the gentle landscape of Orphir, a patchwork of fertile farms by Scapa Flow, is left behind. The crown of the hill is flanked by heather and gorse, with below a panorama of landgirt sea. Moorland falls gently to farmland, bordering the broad bay which divides the Mainland of Orkney from

Hoy Sound from Scorradale. *Charles Tait*

the South Isles. In the middle distance lies Graemsay, where twin lighthouse towers guide shipping past the shoals and crags of Hoy - the 'high island' of the Norse - to the safety of Stromness harbour.

A grid of large, square fields spans the coastal plain. A farm road branches seaward, past some modern houses, to reach the grass-grown drive of the Hall of Clestrain, birthplace of John Rae. The house has been deserted since the 1950s. The wind now whips through broken panes, and pigeons flutter in the shattered interior, but walls of fine-dressed freestone recall an earlier age of elegance.

Two centuries ago, this was the newly-built seat of the Honeyman family, who owned one of Orkney's largest estates. The Orkney lairds of that period had made a fortune from kelp (an essential ingredient of the British glass and soap industries), produced by burning the profuse growth of seaweed around their shores. Smoke from the kelp pits drifted over moorland and moss and the unproductive acres of tenants whose farming methods had changed little in centuries. But Sir William Honeyman, by this time the Lord Advocate Lord Armadale, had put house and estate in the hands of an agricultural improver.

John Rae, Honeyman's estate factor, was a native of Lanarkshire. He and his wife, Margaret Glen Campbell of Argyll, had nine children - five sons and four daughters. (The Glenrae Poultry Farm nearby perhaps commemorates their union.) Their fourth son, John, the future Arctic explorer, was born on 30 September 1813.

When he was barely a year old, the Hall of Clestrain received a visit from Walter Scott, a guest on the yacht of the Northern Lighthouse Commissioners. Scott recorded this impression in his account of the voyage, *Northern Lights, or a Voyage in the Lighthouse Yacht to Nova Zembla and the Lord Knows Where in the Summer of 1814*:

> Mr Rae thinks his example - and he farms very well - has had no effect upon the natives except in the article of potatoes, which they now cultivate a little more...about this time of year all the people turn out for the dogfish, the liver of which affords valuable oil... We saw nineteen boats out at this work.

Scott had noted an aspect of island life which had not yet been eroded by commerce and industry - a dependence on the natural environment for food and other basic necessities. (The islanders had this in common

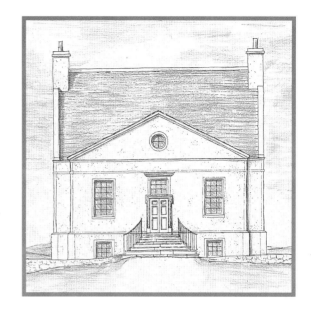

Hall of Clestrain, John Rae's birthplace. Modern reconstruction drawing. *Simpson and Brown*

Opposite: Stenness Loch in winter. *Charles Tait*

Above: Traditional farmhouse, Stronsay, Orkney. *D Horne*

Interior of cottage at Orphir, Orkney, showing central fireplace. *T Kent*

Left: Traditional utensils used in Orkney households in the nineteenth century.

with the Indian tribes of Hudson Bay, and it does much to explain the bond of understanding which arose between them.)

The Orcadians were skilled boatmen, and the fish which they caught were dried for winter consumption. The sea was teeming with coalfish, lythe, haddock and ling. Schools of whales were sometimes 'ca'ed' ashore for the valuable oil obtained from their blubber. Seals, which abounded on the rocky skerries, were also a source of oil; their skins were cured to make footwear and clothing.

The islanders' dwellings were low, windowless structures of turf or stone, shared with livestock and poultry. Smoke from the central hearth drifted through a hole in the roof. Floors were of clay, and beds were stone closets with a mattress of straw or heather - materials used also for thatch, and to make ropes and baskets for use around the farm. Essential household equipment included the rotary quern for grinding meal and malt, and a spinning-wheel to spin yarn for clothing an blankets.

When Rae was a child of six, his father took over the Hudson's Bay Company agency in Stromness. With the arrival of outward bound ships in June, Company officers would have enjoyed the Raes' hospitality. Talk of the 'Nor'wast' must have permeated the household and caught the imagination of the growing boys. Two of John's older brothers, William Glen Rae and Richard (Dick) Rae, joined the Company in 1827 and 1830 respectively. A third brother, Thomas, also went to Canada, setting up business in Hamilton, Ontario. Here, too, a sister, Marion, the wife of Dr James Macaulay Hamilton, settled with her family.

While the Rae children occupied a position of relative wealth and privilege at the Hall of Clestrain, where they were educated by a series of private tutors, their father ensured that the boys, at least, achieved self-reliance through an active outdoor life, which inevitably brought contact with the activities of the native population. In his unpublished autobiography, now in the care of the Scott Polar Research Institute in Cambridge, John Rae wrote:

> My chief and almost sole amusements during vacation or play hours were boating, shooting, fishing and riding (chiefly the three first) all of which my brothers and I had ample opportunities of practising. Two excellent boats were provided for us by our kind father; the one small, light and handy for

Hudson's Bay Company headquarters at Stromness. *Richard Welsby*

9

Fishermen at Rackwick Bay, Hoy, about 1889. *J Valentine.*

fishing and as a sort of tender to the other, which was about 18 feet long and admirably fitted for a crew of boys...

At the shore below the Hall of Clestrain are the remains of the nousts, the boat-shaped, stone-lined hollows where the Raes hauled their craft, and the sailhouse where they stowed their gear. In the larger vessel, the three-masted lug-sailed *Brenda*, the Rae boys sailed 'as long as a stitch of canvas could be carried'. Experience of all conditions of wind and tide was an advantage in their favourite sport of racing other craft, especially the pilot boats of Stromness. Again, from his autobiography:

> It was a grand sight, to see two or three of these racing each other under the impetus of six pairs of powerful arms, against a heavy sea...so as [to be] first to reach a ship in want of a pilot. There was tremendous rivalry between us boys and these brave and experienced boatmen; we had no chance with them in fine weather as they carried no ballast...but whenever it blew hard and the sea was especially rough we never lost an opportunity of racing; and generally went ahead, much to the chagrin of our big opponents...

Despite all this shared activity, Rae remained a sensitive and credulous child. He was the constant victim of hoaxing by his companions, and this encouraged a preference for solitude. He and his brothers had learned to shoot at a very early age, on a small and ancient flint-lock gun. With only the family's Newfoundland dog, Leo, for company, he tramped the surrounding shores and hills in search of game.

The Orkney in which Rae grew up was still largely in its natural state, with broad acres of hill and marshland which, while home to a variety of hardy plants, were devoid of trees. The gently rolling landscape, where the summer sun barely dipped below the horizon, bore a passing resemblance to the Arctic tundra. The youthful Rae shot grouse, snipe, plover, curlew, wild duck, heron, rabbit and seafowl - a supply of game which must have been welcomed by the family. At the 'Bush', the sea outlet of the Stenness Loch, he sometimes caught a dozen or more sea trout, ranging from one to five pounds in weight.

Nowhere could the boy better enjoy outdoor pursuits than on the neighbouring island of Hoy where, unlike the rest of Orkney, the hills appear mountainous and the western seaboard has spectacular cliffs.

At the period of Rae's youth, eagles and ptarmigan still nested there, and men scrambled along the precipices collecting the eggs of seabirds. 'Usually two or three men went in Company so as to aid each other in passing from ledge to ledge, or in lowering one down by a rope from the top of the cliff...'

Self-sufficiency was bred in Rae through the activities of his youth. Apart from shooting and fishing, he observed the seasonal farming work that produced the basic contents of the larder: ploughing, sowing, reaping; then the drying and milling of the grain for bread and ale; the kirning of cream for butter, and the slow maturing of cheese in the Clestrain meal-girnels. All food was home-produced, except for the luxuries of tea and smuggled spirits. Peat was cut and dried in summer, for warmth in winter.

To the solitary pursuits of his childhood, Rae attributed the growth of self-reliance and confidence. Rough walking in wet and cold, sometimes heavily laden with game, built up the physical endurance which characterized his adult life. It had become second nature to him to respond and adapt to the environment, and this was the foundation of Arctic survival. A letter from Rae of 30 June 1875 to R H Major captures an essential aspect of his adaptability:

> We of the Hudson's Bay Company thought very little of our Arctic work. For my own part at least I thought no more of it than any ordinary journey.

EARLY
ARCTIC
EXPLORATION

Ian Bunyan

The great Arctic explorers of the nineteenth century stood at the frontiers of the known world. Like Hillary and Tenzing, Gagarin and Armstrong in the twentieth century, they represented the aspirations of their time. The idea of a north-west passage around the top of America to the Far East is five hundred years old. As early as 1497 John Cabot from Bristol and his son Sebastian, 'discovered' Newfoundland. From this followed a series of voyages to the north-west to try to discover an alternative route to Cathay and the East, the source of many commodities desired by Europe, or a northern way into the Pacific.

Exploration of mainland Canada was pursued by the Portuguese and French while the English opened up Newfoundland to Europeans and made a series of searches for a north-west passage, amongst them three voyages made by John Davis between 1586 and 1588. In the seventeenth century William Baffin, Henry Hudson and Robert Bylot charted the east coast of Baffin Island. Henry Hudson discovered the Bay that bears his name. The area began to be regularly visited by British whalers and the supply ships of the Hudson's Bay Company, founded in 1670, made annual voyages to their fur trading depots. Approaches to the north-west passage from the other side of America had also been made. Vitus Bering explored the straits which were named after him between North America and Asia. In 1778 Captain James Cook got as far as Icy Cape in Alaska (162 w). The Arctic Ocean was reached overland by Samuel Hearne in 1772 and Alexander Mackenzie in 1789 at the Coppermine and Mackenzie Rivers respectively. Nevertheless, by the end of the Napoleonic Wars in 1815 the larger part of the Arctic coastline of Canada remained unknown to Europeans.

Opposite: HMS *Investigator* in pack ice, Beaufort Sea, September 1850. The Franklin search expedition led by Captain McClure. Detail from a watercolour by Samuel Gurney Cresswell.

Why was it that at this time there was a renewed interest in exploration of the far north? In the years 1815-17 whalers returning from the Arctic reported that vast sheets of ice were moving out into the Atlantic and had surrounded the coast of Iceland. Ice stretching from the east coast of Greenland to the north of Spitsbergen which had previously barred entry to the Arctic Ocean for hundreds of years had begun to break up and ships could sail further north than ever before. Moreover, there was ample evidence that there was a sea connection between the northern coasts of North America and Asia. The evidence took the form of tropical driftwood on the shores of West Greenland which could not have come from the Atlantic against the south-west currents prevailing there. That there was a sea connection across the top of America was further suggested by the discovery of harpoons thrown into whales off Greenland in whales killed south of the Bering Straits.

William Scoresby from Whitby, one of the most experienced whaling captains of the time, was dubious as to the value of such a seaway. He wrote 'as affording a navigation to the Pacific Ocean the discovery of a north-west passage could be of no service'. At that time, 1817, the Second Secretary at the Admiralty was the influential John Barrow who had sailed as a whaler to the Arctic and so knew something of the conditions there. He and the President of the Royal Society, Sir Joseph Banks, agreed that it was time to explore the possibility of finding a north-west passage and renewed an earlier incentive, of 1745, by introducing a reward, on a sliding scale, for penetration of the Arctic from west or east, depending on how far the explorers reached. Two thousand pounds was the prize initially offered for achieving completion of the north-west passage. The end of the Napoleonic Wars meant that ships and crews were available to renew the search.

The proposal which was sent to the First Lord of the Admiralty, Lord Melville, was to investigate the geography of the American Arctic, circumnavigate Greenland, find out whether Baffin Bay really existed, and finally to establish if there was a passage from the Atlantic to the Pacific along the north coast of North America.

The first expedition had two main aims: to look for the north-west passage; and to sail towards the North Pole by Spitsbergen. The commander was John Ross, a Scot who was a veteran of Nelson's navy. His

four ships, the flagship *Isabella*, the *Alexander*, the *Trent* and *Dorothea*, were all extensively fitted out for Arctic voyaging. Ross took with him many who were to become famous in polar exploration over the next fifty years. In his own ship there was James Clark Ross, his nephew, then a midshipman. William Parry commanded the *Alexander*; Lieutenant John Franklin commanded the *Trent* with Lieutenant Frederick Beechey as First Officer and George Back as the Admiralty Mate. All were to leave their imprint on the map of the Arctic.

'A remarkable iceberg', 19 June 1818. First Ross expedition. Watercolour by Sir John Ross.

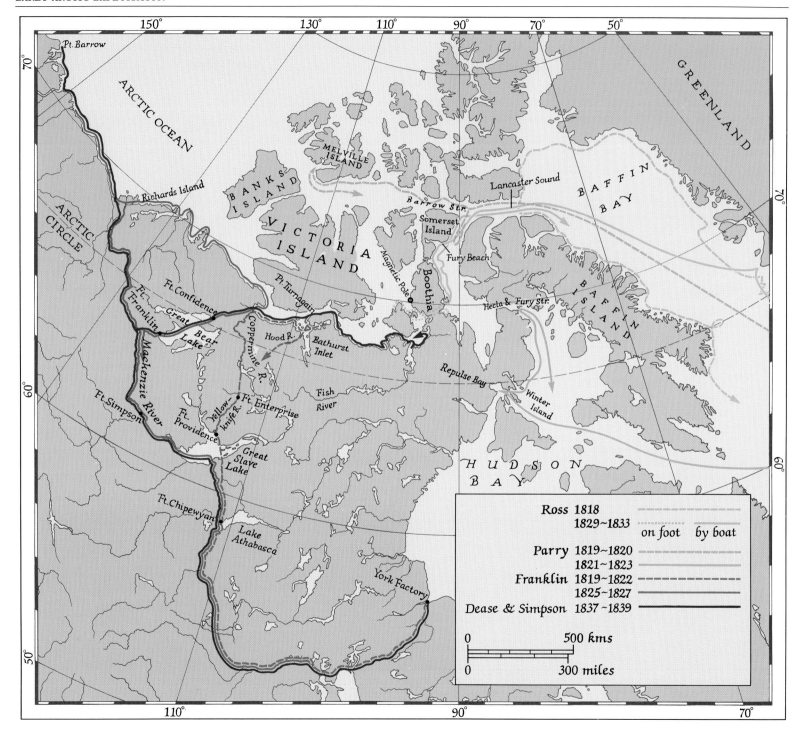

Ross 1818
1829~1833
on foot   by boat

Parry 1819~1820
1821~1823

Franklin 1819~1822
1825~1827

Dease & Simpson 1837~1839

0   500 kms
0   300 miles

The *Isabella* and *Alexander* were to look for the north-west passage, while the *Dorothea* and *Trent* were to head due north towards the pole. Ross's ships sailed up the west coast of Greenland and round the north end of Baffin Bay before entering Lancaster Sound and sailing west until what appeared to be mountains were seen blocking the Sound. Ross decided to turn back, a decision which haunted him later as there were no mountains. He had seen a mirage. On Ross's return Barrow, at the Admiralty, considered that he had not been persistent enough in his search through Lancaster Sound and saw to it that he was not considered for the leadership of an Arctic expedition for the next ten years.

To lead the next attempt, Barrow selected the captain of the *Alexander* in the Ross expedition, William Edward Parry. Parry with the *Hecla* and Lieutenant Matthew Liddon in the *Griper* set out in May 1819, and soon found that there was no obstruction in Lancaster Sound. They were able to sail through its continuation, Barrow Strait, to winter on the south side of Melville Island. The ships' decks were roofed over with tarpaulins, which enabled the crews to exercise and keep fit while they remained trapped in the ice until spring freed the ships. The

The crews of *Hecla* and *Griper* cutting a passage through the ice to Winter Island, 26 September 1819. First Parry expedition.

Opposite: Map showing the Arctic expeditions of Ross and Parry, and Franklin's first two journeys.

17

methods adopted by Parry became standard practice in Arctic exploration for a generation.

Parry's expedition was the most successful of all the Arctic exploring voyages under sail. By reaching Melville Island he was more than half way to the goal of finding a north-west passage. His success encouraged the Admiralty, who were eager that a third attempt should be made, directed further south, particularly along the west side of Hudson Bay. Once again Parry was chosen to command but he took another ship, the *Fury*, captained by Lieutenant George Francis, in place of the slow *Griper*. Many of the officers and men who sailed in the first two expeditions volunteered, including James Clark Ross.

They set out in May 1821 and Parry decided to head for Repulse Bay, but found no channel to the west. Detailed examination of the coast of the Melville Peninsula followed before Parry put his ships into winter quarters at Winter Island. The following summer (1822) was spent surveying the east coast of Melville Peninsula again. From high ground Parry saw the Gulf of Boothia, to the north-west. As signs of scurvy had begun to appear in the crew Parry decided to return home in October 1823, but he was now convinced that the best route westward lay through the Prince Regent Inlet.

Parry's third attempt, again using *Fury* and *Hecla*, saw James Clark Ross and Lieutenant Shere exploring north and south along the west coast of Prince Regent Inlet from a winter base on the eastern shore. When summer freed them they sailed across to Somerset Island and Barrow Strait where Fury went aground and had to be abandoned. Her stores were unloaded and left on the beach. At that point Parry decided to return, arriving home in October 1825. He did not again search for the north-west passage. His last expedition in 1827 struck across the ice from Spitsbergen in an unsuccessful attempt to reach the North Pole.

Meanwhile, John Ross had submitted to the Admiralty a plan for an Arctic expedition using a shallow draft steam vessel to press ahead when winds were adverse. The Admiralty turned him down but eventually Felix Booth of Booth's Gin agreed to help. Ross chose *Victory*, a steam packet which had operated on the Liverpool to the Isle of Man run. She was strengthened for the Arctic and loaded with fuel for a

Meeting the Boothian Inuit, 1829. Watercolour by Sir John Ross. Second Ross expedition.

thousand days. Again, Ross's nephew James Clark Ross was involved, this time as second in command.

They set out on 1 May 1829 and at once problems with the boilers became apparent. *Victory* also leaked. Maximum speed with the engine was only three knots. To cap it all, the crew of the supply ship *John* mutinied. Repairs were necessary, which caused delays, and they did not finally leave Scotland until 13 June, accompanied by a 16 ton boat *Krusenstern*. By 12 August they had reached Prince Regent Inlet and found the place where *Fury*'s stores had been abandoned. The stores were in good condition and some of them were transferred to the *Victory*. By the end of October a suitable winter anchorage was found and *Victory* prepared for the winter. As the weather improved the expedition began to explore the Boothia Peninsula and found that there was no westward passage through the peninsula south of 70°N.

Further exploration to the north was carried out and John Ross crossed over the Boothia Peninsula to reach King William Land (actually an island). By the end of August the ships were still ice-locked and although they managed to move a few miles in September, it was obvious that they were not going to get free that season. Fortunately, the men were all still healthy and survived the winter of 1830 to carry out further exploration in the spring. The greatest achievement of that year was the location of the north magnetic pole by James Clark Ross on 1 June 1831.

Once again, that summer saw hardly any movement of the ships and they prepared to sit out another winter in the ice. During that winter John Ross decided to abandon the ships and set his carpenters to making sledges. Finally, having loaded up with provisions and two boats from the *Victory*, the company set out with the aim of reaching the beach where the remainder of the *Fury*'s stores had been left. They arrived there on 1 July 1832 and Ross then had a base built which he called 'Somerset House'. Two of *Fury*'s boats had survived and they were prepared for sea, leaving *Victory*'s boats behind.

They set out at the end of July, reaching Barrow Strait by early September. It was full of ice so they had to return to Fury Beach, which took another month. A fourth winter, the most severe so far, was then spent in the Arctic. The first man died of scurvy. By 14 August the ice had cleared enough for the remaining men to set out in the boats. Sailing round the top of Baffin Island on the 26 August they came up with the *Isabella* of Hull, by coincidence the same vessel which John Ross had commanded on his first Arctic expedition. They landed at Stromness on 12 October and got back to London a week later.

The successful return of the Ross expedition, which had been given up as lost, brought great honours to John Ross who was knighted and received a lump sum from the Admiralty to cover the back-pay which was owed to his men and which he was unable to pay himself. James Clark Ross was promoted to the rank of Post Captain, but the inquiry that followed the expedition's return brought about a breach between the two men, particularly on the distribution of credit for the achievements of the voyage.

While Edward Parry was making his second attempt to find the northwest passage by sea from the east, an expedition led by Lieutenant John

Franklin, another veteran of Nelson's navy, was sent by the Admiralty overland to 'amend the very defective geography of the northern part of North America'. He was to concentrate on 'the trending of that coast from the Coppermine River to the eastern extremity of that Continent'.

Franklin was accompanied by Dr John Richardson, a Scottish surgeon, and two midshipmen, George Back, who had sailed on Ross's first expedition, and Robert Hood. They set out from London in May 1819 and left the Hudson's Bay Company's base at York Factory on the Bay in September 1819, travelling overland. By the following

York Factory, 1821. Watercolour by Peter Rindisbacher.

21

Building Fort Enterprise, September 1820, first Franklin expedition. Watercolour by Robert Hood.

Franklin's first expedition camped at Point Turnagain. Detail from a watercolour by George Back.

September Franklin had established a base, called Fort Enterprise, near the junction of the Yellowknife and Coppermine Rivers. The expedition spent a very hard winter there. Food was scarce, and they depended on the local Indians to procure meat for them. Eventually in June 1820 Dr Richardson led an advance party north to Point Lake. Franklin followed ten days later with the rest of the expedition to cover the 334 miles to the mouth of the Coppermine River.

The expedition was about twenty strong and consisted of British officers, *voyageurs* (mainly French Canadians), Indians and Inuit. (The Indians and Inuit were to act as interpreters.) The going was very hard at first as their baggage, which included birch bark canoes, had to be dragged over the ice on sledges. They reached the Coppermine River on 2 July and were able to embark on their canoe voyage down the river.

It took almost one month to reach the coast. Then began an epic sea journey by canoe eastwards from the river mouth closely following the coast. They added considerably to their exertions by following the bays and other indentations so that they could map the coast accurately. By the middle of August the deteriorating weather convinced them that it

was time to turn back. Food was becoming short. They were down to a cup of soup and a handful of pemmican (pounded dried meat) per day. The easternmost point reached they called 'Point Turnagain'.

On Little Marten Lake, 1820, first Franklin expedition. Watercolour by Robert Hood.

Their main aim was now to get back to Fort Enterprise before the weather deteriorated much more. Their original intention was to return along the coast and then up the Coppermine, but food was so short that they decided to go up the Hood River, east of the Coppermine. Food was always getting scarcer. At first they were able to kill game but by 20 September they were reduced to eating the bones of long-dead

'Tripe de roche', described by Samuel Hearne, 1795, as 'a black, hard, crumply moss that grows on the rocks'. *Fred Bruemmer*

Reduced to gathering 'tripe de roche' for food, the Barren Lands, 1821. Engraved from a drawing by George Back.

caribou which they found, and even their old shoes. They finally rejoined the Coppermine River on 26 September.

The rest of the journey was a nightmare. In the later stages the party split up, with the slower party led by Richardson. Michel, one of the *voyageurs*, was suspected of killing Hood and another of the *voyageurs*, and also of plotting to kill Hepburn and Richardson. Richardson shot him dead. The quicker party, five men including Franklin, reached Fort Enterprise on 11 October. It was deserted, and worse, no food had been left for them. All they had to eat were deerskins and some lichen ('tripe de roche') growing under the snow.

On 1 November two of the *voyageurs* died of starvation and the four surviving members of the party were in a very weak state. On 7 November three Indians appeared bringing much-needed food but they only stayed for a few days. After another week a much larger party of Indians arrived and preparations to leave Fort Enterprise began. Ten days travel brought them to Fort Providence on the Great Slave Lake. At Moose Deer Island they met Back who had separated from them more than two months earlier. It was he who had sent the Indians to them at Fort Enterprise. He also had his share of privations and at one stage was reduced to eating leather. One of his companions had died.

By the spring the survivors were almost fully recovered and on 26 May 1822 were able to set out for Fort Chipewyan, York Factory and England. News of Franklin's epic journey travelled ahead of him. By the time he was back in England he was already a celebrity. Not long after his return he married Eleanor Porden whom he had known before his expedition but tragically she became fatally ill with tuberculosis.

The second Franklin expedition was also initiated by the Admiralty and again it was overland. This time the main aim was to survey west along the coast from the Mackenzie River to the extreme westernmost point of the North American mainland. Again Dr Richardson volunteered to lead that part of the expedition which was to survey the coast between the Coppermine and Mackenzie Rivers. Lieutenant Back again volunteered and E N Kendall, an Admiralty mate, was appointed as Assistant Surveyor, with Thomas Drummond as Assistant Naturalist. To look after the food, Peter Dease, a Chief Trader of the Hudson's Bay Company, was also taken on. This time, instead of birch bark canoes, Franklin took along mahogany and ash boats, specially built by the Admiralty and more suitable for use on the Arctic Ocean.

Boats in Arctic seas, Franklin's second expedition. Engraved from a drawing by George Back.

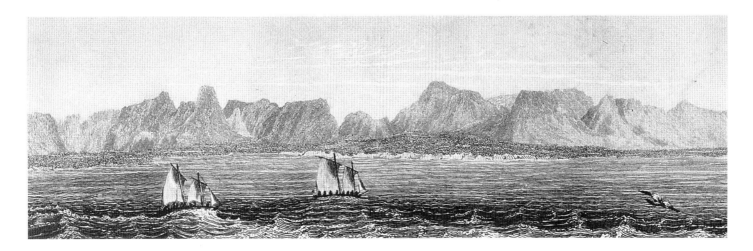

Mountains seen from the Mackenzie River, near Bear Lake. Watercolour by George Back.

Franklin set out from England in February 1825 with Richardson, Back, Kendall, Drummond and four Royal Marines. When they reached America they travelled very quickly across the country, reaching Fort Chipewyan by mid-July. Richardson pressed on ahead almost at once to Fort Resolution on the Great Slave Lake and was joined there by Franklin. By 7 August they reached Fort Norman on the Mackenzie River and Franklin divided his party. His own group set off to reconnoitre the Mackenzie River. Richardson's group was to explore the northern shore of the Great Bear Lake, to the north-east. Franklin's

party reached the sea on 16 August. Contrary winds prevented them sailing west along the coast as planned, so they turned back up the Mackenzie for the winter.

The winter of 1825-6 was spent in comparative comfort in Fort Franklin on Great Bear Lake. With the begining of spring Richardson set out with an Indian guide and a *voyageur* to complete the survey of the Great Bear Lake which he had begun the previous autumn.

Richardson was to rendezvous with Captain F W Beechey in the *Blossom* who had set out to sail into the Arctic from the west. Richardson was to sail back to England on the *Blossom*. If he did not make contact with Beechey's expedition he was to return to Fort Franklin for the winter. Peter Dease was to keep the fort well stocked with food in case Richardson had to winter there. In the meantime, Franklin and Back were to set out with fourteen men in boats built by the carpenters.

The two groups left together on 22 June. At first they were held up by drift ice in the Great Bear River, but they reached Fort Norman at the junction with the Mackenzie River three days later, and continued down the Mackenzie. On 4 July the party divided. Richardson was to survey the area between the Mackenzie and Coppermine Rivers while Franklin set off west along the Arctic coast.

Left: Hare Indians dancing near Fort Franklin, Mackenzie River. Watercolour by George Back.

Right: Panoramic view near Fort Franklin, Great Bear Lake. Deatil from a watercolour by George Back.

Inuit on Richards Island, as a party from Franklin's second expedition approaches, 1826. Engraved from a drawing by E N Kendall, a member of the second Franklin expedition.

Franklin and his men reached the sea on 7 July and almost at once met a large group of Inuit who seemed friendly but then began trying to steal equipment. Back had to threaten to fire on them. Franklin called the place where this happened 'Pillage Point'.

As they progressed along the coast they met other Inuit groups who warned them of the dangers of ice near the coast even in summer. Ice and fog held up their progress. On 27 July Franklin reached what he estimated to be the limit of British territory (Alaska then belonged to the Russian Empire). On 16 August Franklin decided that he had gone as far as he dared that season. He later learned that Beechey's vessel had reached Icy Cape and had sent a party on eastwards with the hope of meeting him. They got as far as Point Barrow, only 160 miles west of Franklin's furthest penetration westwards.

Franklin's party turned back, leaving a message on Foggy Island in case Parry reached that far east. After a rather uncomfortable journey through storms and ice, during which the boats were almost wrecked, they met up with some Inuit who warned them of a plan by some Mountain Indians to kill Franklin's party. They reached the mouth of the Coppermine River unscathed, but found no trace of Richardson's party.

They arrived at Fort Franklin on 21 September. Dr Richardson had already returned but he had set out again by canoe to the Great Slave Lake to work on some geological surveying. Franklin's party had travelled over 2000 miles, Richardson's over 850 miles. They noted that there was nothing to prevent ships getting through as there were plenty of places where they could shelter, but sunken rocks and floating ice would always be a problem.

Franklin concluded his account of this expedition with some observations on the best methods to be used in opening the north-west passage. He hoped that Great Britain would not 'relax her efforts until the question of a north-west passage has been satisfactorily set at rest or at least until those portions of the northern shores of America, which are as yet unknown, be laid down on our maps'.

For the next few years Franklin was fully occupied producing his report on the expedition. He remarried, this time Jane Griffin, herself a keen traveller, and with her he visited Russia. He was knighted - Dr Richardson received a knighthood later. After a period in the Mediterranean and as Governor of Van Dieman's Land (Tasmania) Franklin returned to England in 1843.

Popular interest in Arctic exploration had waned but work was still going on. In 1836 George Back led an expedition in HMS *Terror* to trace the coast between Repulse Bay and Point Turnagain. Employees of the Hudson's Bay Company did much to fill the unknown parts of the map. The next year Peter Dease and Thomas Simpson reached beyond Franklin's furthest point west. They then set out from Fort Confidence on the Great Bear Lake in 1838 and proceeded along the coast from the

Small boats in a gale in Arctic waters. Watercolour by George Back.

The Barren Lands, 1826, difficult terrain which many Arctic expeditions encountered. Engraved from a drawing by E N Kendall.

Opposite: Bathurst Inlet today, in September. Bathurst Inlet, between the mouth of the Coppermine and Kent Peninsula, was visited by several expeditions. *I K MacNeil*

Coppermine River towards Bathurst Inlet. The following season they again went down the Coppermine and on to the mouth of Back's River. Most important, they learned the skills of travelling light and quickly, living off the land as the native peoples were accustomed to do.

In 1844 the redoubtable Sir John Barrow urged the First Lord of the Admiralty to authorize one more attempt to find a north-west passage. The Admiralty agreed and proposed the best equipped expedition that had ever ventured into the Arctic. Sir James Clark Ross was exhausted by his recent Antarctic voyage and refused to go. Sir John Franklin was the next logical choice as the man who had explored most of the Arctic coast. He was of an older generation and doubts were expressed about the wisdom of sending a man of fifty-nine to lead such an expedition. But with his great prestige and influence these doubts were soon silenced. He was appointed in February 1845 with orders to sail through Lancaster Sound and Barrow Strait as far as Cape Walker, then to proceed south and west in as straight a line as allowed by the ice or any unknown land, toward Bering Strait.

He was to use *Erebus* and *Terror*, well proved in the Antarctic by Sir James Clark Ross. This time they were to be fitted with auxiliary steam engines (actually railway engines adapted to drive screw propellers). *Erebus*, Franklin's ship, had a crew of sixty-seven officers and men and *Terror*, commanded by Captain Crozier, had a crew of sixty-two. They had supplies for three years. Much of the food was in tins, a fairly recent innovation. Franklin said that no one should worry if they did not return within three years. The expedition sailed in June 1845, put in at Disco in Greenland and was last seen by whalers in Baffin Bay.

Two years passed and nothing was heard. Nobody was unduly worried, although Dr Richard King, who had travelled with Captain Back on the Great Fish River in 1833 (later renamed Back's River), suggested that an expedition be sent immediately to look in the area of Back's River mouth. By 1847 Lady Franklin began to be anxious and started her heroic efforts, which lasted for thirteen years, to encourage the rescue of the expedition.

She began by writing to the Prime Minister, Lord Palmerston, the Emperor of France, the Czar of Russia and the President of the United States, asking them to send ships to rescue the expedition. The British Government responded by asking the Hudson's Bay Company to send supplies to their most northerly posts. Officials were to tell the Indians to look out for white men coming in from the north. Northern whalers were also alerted and offered a reward for information.

When in 1848 there was still no news, the British Government sent three search expeditions. Sir James Clark Ross commanded in HMS *Enterprise* which, with HMS *Investigator*, followed Franklin's intended route. Three other ships were sent up the west coast of America to search along the coast of the Arctic Ocean beyond the Bering Strait. Sir John Richardson, Franklin's old friend and colleague, was ordered to search down the Mackenzie River east of the Coppermine.

He took with him John Rae. Rae already had ten years experience of the Canadian Arctic, and had proved his self-sufficiency and ability to hunt, fish, sledge and use snowshoes. Rae had previously led an expedition to survey the Arctic coast and had travelled almost as far as Fury and Hecla Strait, ably demonstrating that Europeans could be self-supporting in the very harsh environment.

The expedition of 1848-9, although it added considerably to knowledge of the Arctic, found no trace of Franklin. Rae made a second search in 1851, and got very near to where the final episode of the Franklin tragedy was later shown to have occurred, but he found nothing to help solve the mystery.

The year 1850 saw the most intense search. A £20,000 reward was offered by the British Government. In August Captain Erasmus Omanney and officers of his search ship HMS *Assistance* found signs of Franklin's expedition on Devon Island. Soon afterwards, on Beechey Island, only a mile and a quarter away, the site of Franklin's first winter base was found by Captain Penny and the crew of HMS *Lady*

The Arctic Council planning the search for Sir John Franklin, 1851. Sir George Back and Sir William Parry (with white hair) are on the left. Sir John Richardson points to the chart on the table. Sir James Clark Ross (not in uniform) stands beneath a portrait of Franklin. Oil painting by Stephen Pearce.

Franklin. There were the remains of tent sites, a storehouse and a carpenters' house. From the evidence it seemed that all had been going well during the winter of 1845, though the graves of three young crew members suggested that at some point there were difficulties.

By this time fifteen ships and five hundred men were searching in northern waters, though still not in the area suggested by Dr King. One expedition was equipped by the Hudson's Bay Company and commanded by Rear Admiral Sir John Ross in the yacht *Felix*. Another was financed by the people of Tasmania and Lady Franklin. Lady Franklin spent most of her personal fortune financing these search expeditions. She was helped by a wealthy New York merchant Henry Grinell, who bought two schooners and turned them over to the United States Navy. The officers and men on these ships signed a bond renouncing any claim to a reward.

The British Government also sent five ships in 1850 under overall command of Sir Edward Belcher. Belcher's ships also looked for McClure and Collinson: *Enterprise* and *Investigator* had not been seen since 1850 when they had sailed east through the Bering Strait. HMS *Enterprise* got as far as Cambridge Bay and then sailed for home, but in 1851 *Investigator* got stuck in the ice off the north-east coast of Banks Island.

In February 1853 McClure abandoned *Investigator* and was trying to find help when he ran into the Belcher expedition. After a fourth winter on the ice, McClure's party went on board a Royal Navy search ship which had come into the area. In all six ships were abandoned in the ice that year. One of them, the *Resolute,* drifted a thousand miles eastwards where she was recovered by an American whaler. McClure's men were acknowledged as the first to complete the north-west passage from west to east and for this they received £10,000 from the British Government.

It was Rae's fourth and last Arctic journey in 1853-4 that led to the first conclusive evidence of Franklin's fate. Rae and his men wintered at Repulse Bay and then went on to Committee Bay and Pelly Bay on the east side of the Boothia Peninsula. Near the head of Pelly Bay they encountered a group of Inuit, and some time later met a solitary Inuit who provided the first news of Franklin. He said that thirty-five to forty

Opposite: HMS *Investigator*, McClure search expedition, trapped in pack ice, 1850-51. Detail from a colour lithograph from a drawing by Lt Samuel Gurney Cresswell.

Inuit men of Igloolik, drawn by Capt.
Lyon of HMS *Hecla*, 1821.

Kabloonans (white men) had starved to death west of a large river a
long way away (ten to twelve days' journey). Dead bodies had been
seen beyond two large rivers. Rae thought that the information was too
vague to act on but he bought a gold cap band from the man and asked
him to tell his friends of his interest. Rae's subsequent travels took him
to the mouth of the Castor and Pollux Rivers where there was a cairn
built by Dease and Simpson in 1839, then on to the west coast of the
Boothia Peninsula where he did not complete his survey. On the return
journey to Repulse Bay Rae's party again met the Inuit and Rae obtained more objects which had belonged to Franklin's men.

At Repulse Bay Rae was visited by more Inuit bringing yet more
relics. From the end of May until August he was able to question them
quite closely about what they had heard. It emerged that while hunting
seals near the shore of King William Island four winters ago (Rae then
thought 1850) a group of Inuit had met about forty men travelling south
over the ice dragging a boat and sledges. The men were thin and thought
to be short of food. They were hoping to find caribou to shoot. Later the
same season the bodies of thirty men and some graves were discovered
on the mainland and five dead bodies on an island (Rae thought probably Montreal Island) a long day's journey to the north-west of a large
river (probably Back's River). Some of the bodies were in a tent or tents,
others under a boat. Rae bought some of the articles which the Inuit had
collected. These included silver plate marked with Franklin's name,
Franklin's Order of Hanover and several silver forks and spoons with
initials or crests of officers from the ill-fated expedition.

When Rae returned to England in August he reported to the Admiralty on his findings. He added to his report 'From the mutilated state
of many of the corpses and the contents of the kettles it is evident that
our wretched countrymen had been driven to the last recourse - cannibalism - as a means of prolonging existence.'

The Admiralty accepted Rae's report though many people, especially those who knew nothing of life in the far north, did not. Sir John
Richardson and Sir John Ross were among his supporters. Rae refused
at that stage to lead another expedition to verify his findings.

One of Rae's severest critics was Dr King, probably because he had
hoped to be the person to find out about the Franklin expedition. Rae

Hauling sledges, with some help from the wind. Belcher expedition, 1850, drawn by W W May.

was criticized for believing what he was told by the Inuit - regarded by many as an unreliable source of information. But he knew them very well and had plenty of time at Repulse Bay to glean all the information they could provide. He was blamed for not going to check for himself at the place where the Inuit said it all happened. But it was clear that Rae only heard the full story after he had reached Repulse Bay and it was too late in the season for him to go back, and in any case he could not have done anything for Franklin's men. And Rae's expedition always had the primary purpose of trying to complete the coastal survey.

Rae was also accused of being in too much of a hurry to rush back to England to claim the reward, but he insisted that he did not know of the reward until his return to England. Finally, the Victorian public refused to believe that a crew of British officers and men could resort to cannibalism. Rae himself was more tolerant. He had experienced the extremes of hunger which drove men to cannibalism and had known of other cases at Hudson's Bay Company outposts.

In November 1854 the Governor of the Hudson's Bay Company wrote to the Admiralty claiming the reward for Rae and his men. Rae was having an argument with the Company as they would not pay him for undertaking the expedition anything over and above his salary as a factor. When Rae himself wrote to the Admiralty claiming the reward they referred it to their solicitor. He agreed to give a decision in three months, but news of another overland expedition led by James Anderson of the Hudson's Bay Company prompted him to wait until he had seen Anderson's report.

The report was received in January 1856. Anderson had canoed down the Fish River and spent nine days in August 1856 searching Montreal Island and the west shore of Chantrey Inlet. He found the remains of a broken-up boat and other material clearly from the missing ships. He also met Inuit who knew something but as he had no interpreter with him he could not add anything significant to Rae's evidence.

The assessment of Rae's claim brought further criticism in the form of anonymous pamphlets. These again challenged him on the grounds that he had not visited the site described by the Inuit and reiterated that they were unreliable witnesses. Finally, his statement about cannibalism was again called into question.

Rae replied by sending his field notes to the Admiralty, which showed just how vague the early information about the site of the tragedy had been. He pointed out from his own knowledge of Franklin's previous much shorter but disastrous overland expeditions with much smaller parties that it was very unlikely that Franklin would have taken a route which would involve travelling six hundred miles to the nearest Hudson's Bay Company post. Much more likely was the better-known route via Fury Beach, already travelled by the Rosses in 1832-5.

Lady Franklin also opposed the award to Rae, and communicated her feelings to the Admiralty in April 1856. She considered it premature to reward Rae as he had found only general details of the expedition's fate. There might be more to discover and an award could discourage others from looking. Rae was anxious for a decision, and in May 1856 rather impatiently again approached the Admiralty. There had been other claimants. Dr King's claim was on the grounds that he had said they should have looked in the Great Fish River and King William Island area all along. William Penny, the captain of HMS *Lady Franklin*, also claimed. Finally, in June 1856, the Admiralty solicitor told Rae and the Secretary of the Hudson's Bay Company that Rae and his companions should have the reward but the Company was to decide how it was to be divided.

Rae received £8000 and the men who had been at Pelly Bay in 1853-4 shared £2000. That was all the monetary reward that went to Rae. He was the only significant contributor to the search for Franklin who was not knighted.

Rae's evidence was enough to convince the British Government that no further expeditions need be sent, but Lady Franklin did not give up. She tried for two more years to persuade the Prime Minister that the search should go on. Eventually, she bought the 200 ton steam yacht *Fox*, had it strengthened for the ice, and appointed Captain Leopold McClintock as commander. He sailed in July 1857 with a crew of twenty-seven.

The *Fox* did not have an easy passage, getting stuck in the ice off Leicester Sound and drifting for eight months. McClintock reached Beechey Island in the summer of 1858 and erected a monument to Franklin and his men. Establishing a winter base at the eastern end of Bellot Strait, he sent out sledging parties in February 1859. McClintock travelled down the west coast of the Boothia Peninsula. Near Cape Victoria he met a party of about forty-five Inuit who told him that they too had relics of the Franklin expedition, more spoons, buttons and other equipment. One of them told him that a ship had sunk off King William Island but that the crew had landed safely. In April McClintock set out again on the east coast of King William Island. His second in

Lady Jane Franklin, 1876. Chalk vignette by Amélie Munier Romilly.

Map showing Franklin's last expedition
and the search expeditions of McClure
and McClintock.

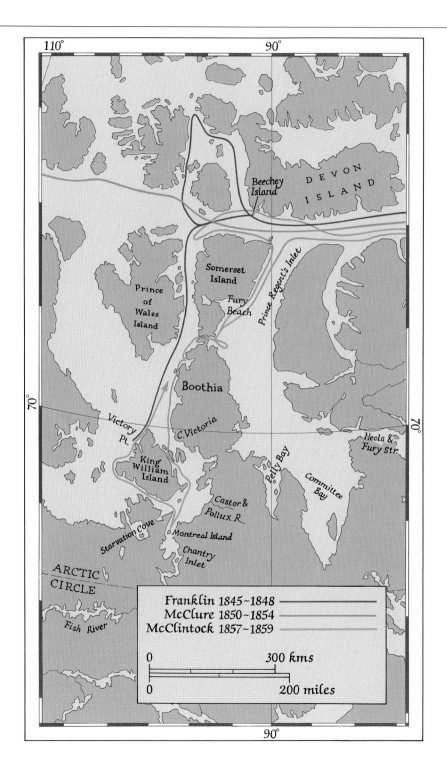

DEVON ISLAND

Beechey Island

Somerset Island

Prince Regent's Inlet

Prince of Wales Island

Fury Beach

Boothia

Victory Pt.

C. Victoria

Hecla & Fury Str.

King William Island

Pelly Bay

Committee Bay

Castor & Pollux R.

Starvation Cove

Montreal Island

Chantry Inlet

ARCTIC CIRCLE

Fish River

Franklin 1845~1848 ————
McClure 1850~1854 ————
McClintock 1857~1859 ————

0   300 kms

0   200 miles

command William Hobson explored the west coast of the island while a third group investigated Prince of Wales Island.

On King William Island McClintock met some of the Inuit he had encountered earlier. They now told him that two ships had been seen. One had sunk but the other had been forced up on the ice. Further down the coast McClintock met another group of Inuit who said they had visited the wrecked ship. From them he bought pieces of silver plate on which were crests belonging to Franklin, Crozier and other officers, together with more buttons. The Inuit said there were many books on the ship. They also described how many of the white men had fallen and died as they walked. Some had been buried, others had not.

A few days later, while walking along a gravel ridge near the beach on the south shore of King William Island, McClintock found the skeleton of a young crewman. He then continued up the west coast of King William Island, following Hobson who had returned ahead of him to the *Fox*. A note from Hobson said that he himself had found a note of May 1847 left by a party from *Erebus* and *Terror*, telling how they had wintered on Beechey Island and turned into Wellington Channel. All was then well. A second message had been added to the same piece of paper a year later, which told of the death of Sir John Franklin in June 1847 and the abandoning of *Erebus* and *Terror* in April 1848. The ships had been stuck in the ice since September 1846. A large group of men, 105 in all, had passed King William Island on 25 April 1848 on their way to the Fish River. Nine officers and fifteen men had died up to that time.

On the way back to the *Fox* more personal relics were found in a large boat and sledge, with the skeletons of two men. There were two strange things about that boat. Firstly, it was pointing *back* towards the north, as if it was being hauled back towards the abandoned ships, and secondly the contents of the boat, towels, soap, silk handkerchiefs, sponges, shoes, nails, files, books, large spoons, forks and even teaspoons with more officers' crests, amounted to a very heavy load, even for a group of men who were in the best of health. Further on, a note from Hobson described how he had discovered more non-essentials scattered about, heavy cooking stoves, pick axes, and so on.

McClintock's findings essentially bore out Rae's story, but since then there have been more expeditions. In 1869 and 1879 the Americans

Opening the cairn at Victory Point, where Captain McClintock's search expedition found a message telling of Franklin's death, 1859. *Illustrated London News*

The Schwatka expedition meeting Inuit. John Rae's meetings with Inuit yielded crucial information about the fate of Franklin. Drawing by W Klutschak, 1879.

C F Hall and F Schwatka came to the area. In 1925-30 Major Burwash located Crozier's landing place near Victory Point. H A Larsen of the Royal Canadian Mounted Police explored from Collinson Inlet to Cape Felix in 1949. As recently as 1967 the Canadian Government mounted a search as part of Project Franklin.

Hall and Schwatka found evidence to suggest that the Inuit reached the ships. Further research has helped to pinpoint the site of the final tragedy more closely to where the Inuit said thirty bodies were found. The suggestion is now that it was probably a bay on the Adelaide Peninsula (now called Starvation Cove) as several skeletons were found there and also on one of the Todd Islands off the south coast of King William Island. Anderson found the remains of a boat on Montreal Island but it now seems likely that they were taken there by Inuit.

In 1981 Dr Owen Beattie made a survey of King William Island looking for Franklin relics. At Booth Point he found some human bones which were likely to have belonged to one of the ill-fated crew. Apart from showing signs of scurvey, the bones also revealed unusually high levels of lead. Beattie thought that this might have been caused by lead poisoning from the lead solder used in the expedition's canned food supplies, from the lead foil in which tea and chocolate were wrapped, or the lead-glazed pottery which the crew were known to have used.

In an attempt to verify these high lead levels in the bones Beattie arranged in 1984 and 1986 to exhume the only members of the Franklin expedition whose graves were known, the three buried on Beechey Island in 1846. The bodies of the three men were found to have been very well preserved in the permafrost and the amount of lead was very much above normal (138-313 parts per million). It was suggested that this was enough to have contributed to their weakness and eventual death from pneumonia or tuberculosis. There was a heap of tin cans left behind at the winter camp on Beechey Island. Investigation showed that many of these were poorly made and might not have protected the food from decay. The result of this was that the food stores on *Erebus* and *Terror*, originally thought more than adequate for the voyage, might have begun to run out, forcing abandonment of the ships in 1848. Moreover, Beattie considered it more than likely that the expedition was showing signs of lead poisoning, fatigue, weakness and even paralysis, by the time they abandoned the ships. The mental state of the crew may go some way to explain some of the strange finds made by the searchers, especially the large amounts of superfluous equipment.

Further investigation and the piecing together of evidence may help to shed more light on the last days of Franklin and his men. But there is already a wealth of evidence to illustrate the inspiring courage and determination of the men who explored the Arctic. An important and moving aspect of the story concerns the learning of basic lessons of survival. The Arctic was harsh and hostile to those who brought to it the ways of a very different environment, but for men like Rae, prepared to adapt and understand, it offered a challenge that came within the bounds of rational human effort.

The body of John Torrington, one of Franklin's crew, excavated by Owen Beattie in 1986. *Owen Beattie*

RAE
IN THE
ARCTIC

Jenni Calder

John Rae was twenty years old when he sailed from Stromness as surgeon to the *Prince of Wales*, the Hudson's Bay Company's supply ship. Thirty-one other Orkneymen left with him, to enter the service of the Hudson's Bay Company. They were bound for Moose Factory, the Company's post in James Bay, an inlet of Hudson Bay. It was a natural departure for Rae. He had spent four years in Edinburgh studying medicine, first at the university and then at Surgeon's Hall, and this combined with his rugged upbringing equipped him well for the job. It equipped him even more effectively for what the future actually brought, which may have reflected his hopes rather more accurately than the job of ship's surgeon. Rae's response to his first experience of Arctic seas is recorded in his autobiography and illustrates both the beauty and the boredom of the world he had entered.

> Perhaps there is nothing that strikes a person more forcibly than the first sight of Icebergs and floe ice. The beauty, and purity, vastness and variety of the former are so attractive that you feel at first as if you could never weary of seeing and admiring them, yet to lie for weeks along side of almost the same floe began to pall, and we all wished a change of some kind.

Ice was also a danger, and had proved the greatest impediment to Arctic exploration, but Rae learned that it could be both enemy and ally. As with most features of the Arctic environment, understanding and experience were the clues to learning to live with it.

It was certainly ice that changed the course of Rae's career. The *Prince of Wales* was on her homeward voyage when her progress was blocked by ice in Hudson Strait. There was no option but to turn back and winter near Moose Factory. Far from regretting this enforced stay,

Opposite: Crossing a reef, 1826. Travelling Arctic rivers and lakes in small boats entailed frequent portages. Detail from an engraving after a drawing by George Back.

The Hudson's Bay Company supply ship *Prince of Wales* striking rocks in Hudson Straits, 7 August 1819. Detail from a watercolour by Robert Hood, midshipman on the first Franklin expedition.

Rae accepted an offer from George Simpson to become 'surgeon and clerk' at Moose Bay for five years. In the event, he stayed for ten, and although his stated preference was to be employed as a doctor, his natural abilities and interests soon involved him in other aspects of Hudson Bay life and work.

In that ten years Rae built on his youthful training in Orkney. His autobiography provides a self-portrait of a purposeful and practical young man, driven by a pragmatic curiosity and a clear dislike of inactivity. His services as surgeon were not much required, which left him time for hunting, travelling and getting to know the local Indians. He proved himself a quick learner, from observation and experience, and demonstrated a striking talent for improvisation. He developed and refined the skills he had been introduced to as a boy, and adopted new ones - snowshoe walking, for example, and sledging. These activities were encouraged by the Company; at an early stage he was identified as having much to contribute to the territory.

Rae lost no opportunity to investigate the land and its wildlife. In his readiness to experiment and adapt he was like many of the Scots who feature so significantly in the history of the Hudson's Bay Company and of the opening up of Canada. But the degree to which he was prepared to test himself was exceptional, and the cool understatement that characterizes his accounts of his adventures is striking. On one occasion, when on a hunting trip with George Rivers, a Cree Indian whose hunting skills he much admired, Rae had to plunge into freezing water to retrieve a canoe. 'I had to wade waist deep in water covered with an inch of snow,' he recounted, 'there being no handy opportunity of changing clothes or drying myself, (it was freezing pretty hard), I was not quite comfortable.'

During these ten years, Admiralty-initiated exploration in Arctic waters continued, spurred by the belief that the enigma of the northwest passage was on the brink of solution. But much of the most valuable work of exploration and surveying was carried out on land, in particular by two Hudson's Bay Company employees, Peter Warren Dease and Thomas Simpson, a cousin of Sir George Simpson. Whatever the motives of the Admiralty in pursuing the search for a route through to the Pacific, those of the Company in exploring and mapping

the north and west of the continent were pragmatic. The influence and continuing commercial success of the Company were well served by the accumulating knowledge of the geography and the people of the 209,000 square miles of Company territory. In the course of going about their normal duties, the employees acclimatized themselves to hard winters and hard travelling. The need for self-sufficiency bred an independence and adaptability which was often lacking amongst the officers and men of naval expeditions, and made Company men good material for the challenge of Arctic exploration.

Moose Factory, the Hudson's Bay Company post in James Bay, 1854. Lithograph from a sketch by W Trask.

Sir George Simpson, Governor in Chief of the Hudson's Bay Company territories, 1856. Oil painting by Stephen Pearce.

Opposite: Repulse Bay in summer, Rae's base for exploration further north. *Fred Bruemmer*

Dease and Simpson were in many ways the immediate precursors to the next phase of Rae's career. Their expedition of 1837-9 charted stretches of the Arctic coast west of the mouth of the Mackenzie River and east of Turnagain Point, which Franklin and Richardson had reached in 1826. They filled in significant gaps, but deteriorating weather prevented them from fulfilling their aim to establish whether Boothia Peninsula was attached to the mainland. Simpson thought it was an island. The verification, or otherwise, of this was a major objective of Rae's subsequent journeys.

The survey of the northern coast remained to be completed, and in 1844 Sir George Simpson identified John Rae as the man to carry out the final stage of the task. Simpson was well aware of what Arctic travel entailed and confident that Rae was the right man. Rae would, however, have to learn the techniques of surveying. To do so, he walked from Hudson Bay to Red River, then, when he found that his appointed tutor was too ill to instruct him, to Sault Ste Marie on Lake Superior - 1200 miles on snowshoes. He continued, still on foot, to Toronto, where he got the instruction he needed. Even for a man used to snowshoeing fifty miles in a day this was a considerable journey.

Rae's brief was, according to Simpson's instructions, 'to complete the geography of the northern shore of America'. He was also expected to make detailed observations on botany, zoology and geology, as well as the ethnography of the Inuit. It was assumed at the start that he might have to winter in the Arctic. While he was preparing for this expedition he was encountered by the novelist R M Ballantyne, at that time also a Bay employee. 'He was very muscular and active,' Ballantyne wrote, 'full of animal spirits, and had a fine intellectual countenance. He was considered, by those who knew him well, to be one of the best snow-shoe walkers in the service, was also an excellent rifle-shot, and could stand an immense amount of fatigue.'

Rae set off on 5 July 1846 by boat from Churchill, north of Moose Factory, to Repulse Bay, just within the Arctic Circle. He had with him a dozen men, including Orcadians, French Canadians, a Cree Indian and two Inuit, Ouligbuck father and son. It took nearly three weeks to reach Repulse Bay, which became their base for exploration further north. During what remained of the brief summer they crossed Rae

John Rae. A photograph probably taken in the 1840s.

Isthmus to Committee Bay and explored both to the north-west and the north-east, up the west coast of Melville Peninsula. Although he was not able to confirm this, Rae formed the opinion that Boothia was not an island but attached to the mainland. But already by 11 August the caribou were migrating south. Winter was closing in and Rae was forced to give up further travelling.

Rae's preparations for the winter included the building of a large stone house with a roof improvised from oars, masts, oilcloth and moose skins, hunting and gathering fuel. It was vital to lay in sufficient food and fuel to get them through the winter. All the time Rae continued his observations, of the weather, the movement of ice, and, in great detail, the wildlife. He also took every opportunity to talk with any Inuit encountered, to learn from them about the topography and the movement of game, and to pick up any tips that might be useful - indeed, vital - to survival.

Even when completely beset by winter conditions Rae and his men kept busy, but always with an eye to health and the practical needs of food and shelter. He encouraged his men to acquire native techniques of providing shelter, and always took the lead, never asking of his men anything that he would not undertake himself. Much of his pragmatism was common sense, but a common sense that was sometimes lacking amongst those who undertook Arctic travel. His autobiography

The ruins of Fort Hope, the stone shelter built by Rae and his men at Repulse Bay. Photographed in 1933.

Opposite: Wager Bay, near Repulse Bay.

provides fascinating evidence of daily activities:

> We now had no encouragement to move much about, as there was no game to be seen and the weather was very unsettled, and consequently no more exercise was taken than was necessary to keep us in good health. In stormy weather, not being able to get out of doors, the men wrestled or played some game which called the muscles into action, and thus kept up the animal heat.

Inside, the temperature could be as low as 40° below freezing - 'some few degrees more heat would have been preferable,' Rae comments - and when the weather was so bad that the men could not go out for water they were able to cook only one meal a day. But on the whole they were well supplied with food. On Christmas Day they played football and ate a good dinner of venison, plum pudding and 'a moderate allowance of brandy punch'. On New Year's Day there were hare and currant pudding.

Early in April Rae and a small group of men were ready to set off again on their travels, measuring and surveying as they went. During the winter dogs had been purchased from the Inuit and they were now travelling with dog sledges. They spent a month, struggling through bad weather, gradually filling in some of the gaps on the map. After a

Sledge and dog team. Rae sometimes travelled in similar style. *Fred Bruemmer*

week back at Repulse Bay, Rae set out again, heading north up the west coast of Melville Peninsula. It was a gruelling journey.

> At one moment we sank nearly waist-deep in snow, at another we were up to our knees in salt water, and then again upon a piece of ice so slippery that, with our wet and frozen shoes it was impossible to keep from falling. Sometimes we had to crawl out of a hole on all fours like some strange-looking quadrupeds...

Their goal was Hecla and Fury Strait but they did not quite make it, reaching Cape Crozier, about ten miles to the south. Food and fuel (on occasion, they burned some of their alcohol supply as fuel) were dangerously scarce, and they turned for home.

Bad weather kept them at Repulse Bay, and it was the end of August before they arrived back at Churchill. The task Rae had accomplished was considerable, although it was not quite all that had been hoped for. In surveying 625 miles of unexplored coastline, he was able to confirm that there was no sea connection between Hudson Bay and the west and to establish, at least to his own satisfaction, that Boothia was not an island. But perhaps more remarkably, he and his men had spent fifteen months in the Arctic, largely self-sufficient, and all had returned in good health, in spite of suffering from frostbite which blackened the skin and privation which left them 'very much reduced in flesh'.

Rae continued on to England, where he reported on the expedition to the board of the Hudson's Bay Company. His presence in London coincided with mounting concern over the fate of Sir John Franklin and the *Erebus* and *Terror*. Nothing had been heard of the expedition for over two years. One of the strongest advocates of sending out a search expedition was Sir John Richardson, Franklin's companion on the epic explorations of 1819-22, who believed it possible that Franklin, if forced to make his way south, would have travelled up the Mackenzie River. Richardson, also a Scot and trained at Edinburgh as a surgeon and naturalist, was requested to lead one arm of the search. Richardson was already well advanced in his preparations when he wrote to Rae, asking him to be his second in command. He recognized the value of Rae's skill and experience, although it was evident that there was a coolness in relations between the Admiralty and the more rugged and commercial Hudson's Bay Company. Sir George

Sir John Richardson. Oil painting by
Stephen Pearce.

Simpson took a critical view of the Admiralty expeditions to the north,
but he gave practical help to Richardson and Rae.

Richardson was much older than Rae, and was, of course, a naval
man. But although Rae was from time to time given to sardonic com-
ment about Sir John, he warmly acknowledged his qualities. 'He was
one of the most conscientious and honourable men that ever lived,' he
wrote, '...a sincere and true Christian', cultured, and extremely well-
informed on scientific matters:

> Everything animate or inanimate, from the smallest shrub to the largest
> tree, from the tomtit to the swan, from the most minute dweller in the water
> to the great whale, all quadrupeds and insect life in their numerous vari-
> eties, the composition of the strata of our world from the simplest [?] to the
> most interesting fossil bearing rocks, were all more or less well known to
> him, and he had something interesting or instructive to say of each or of any
> of them when met with.

Rae was well aware of the value of such knowledge, for in addition to
its contribution to science the ability to 'read' the environment could
be a matter of life and death. Although Rae had been brought up to
observe landscape, climate and wildlife, and had already shown how
crucial this was to Arctic survival, he readily acknowledged how much
he learnt from Richardson.

Rae was impatient of naval protocol and the gentlemen officers
whose courage and scientific abilities could never make up for ignorance of the Arctic environment and its demands. The Admiralty had
conscripted a mixed group of servicemen from England (who were,
Rae felt, not 'very well fitted for what they have to go through') and
locally recruited men. The servicemen had neither the strength nor the
stamina to match the Bay men (nor, it seemed, commitment), as this
description of portage work, again from the autobiography, indicates:

> The men were also not good at portage work as they carried light loads cer-
> tainly...not half what the Hudson's Bay men would do, and this doubled
> the distance and lost time. I felt so annoyed at seeing a great strong man
> walking off with perhaps one or at most, two oars on his shoulder, that occa-
> sionally I used to take up all the oars, the mast, and poles of a boat at one
> time, not a heavy load, and carry them over the portage with ease. This had
> some little effect but not much.

Left to right: Walrus, red fox, Arctic willow, lousewort, osprey, poppy. Rae would have been familiar with all of these. *W Lynch*

It is clear that Rae was not averse to demonstrating his own abilities - but what was at issue was not competitiveness, but survival.

One of the Hudson's Bay men was of particular value to Rae. John Corrigal was also from Orphir, Rae's birthplace, and was for a while stationed at Moose Factory. When Rae left Moose in April 1844 Corrigal was with him, and he was recruited for the expedition as steersman. There were times when Corrigal was Rae's only companion, and he is frequently mentioned in Rae's accounts.

The expedition made the long journey by canoe and portage down the Mackenzie River, along the coast and overland to Great Bear Lake. There they established a base at Fort Confidence. Although the primary purpose of the expedition was to search for Franklin, equally

Fort Confidence in winter, 1850-1. Watercolour and pen and ink by John Rae.

Opposite: Mackenzie River delta.

important were the opportunities for scientific observation, collecting zoological specimens and filling in the map. The following summer, 1849, Richardson returned to England, leaving Rae to continue the search, particularly in the Wollaston Land area, but his way was impeded by pack ice and he had to give up. On the return journey to Fort Confidence an Inuit interpreter was drowned, the only man Rae lost on any of his expeditions.

Although Rae and Richardson had added to knowledge of the Arctic coast they had failed to determine the fate of Franklin and his men. 'I am sorry to say,' Rae wrote to Sir George Simpson, 'that we have been quite unsuccessful in the object of our voyage.' Concern for the fate of Franklin did not dwindle with time, and plans were soon being developed for more intensive searching. Inevitably, as the Company continued its involvement in the search, Rae was again recruited to play a part in this.

While engaged on this expedition, Rae had been appointed by the Bay as Chief Factor at Fort Simpson, in charge of the Mackenzie River District. He took up his new post in the autumn of 1849 and tried to settle down to a fur-trading life, but it was difficult to adjust to a more routine existence after the challenge and rigours of Arctic travel. His duties involved supervising the collection of skins from Indians and traders, payment, and equipping further trapping and trade. Although knowledge of the territory and a sympathetic understanding of people were assets, for a man like Rae there was no great challenge. However, it was less than a year before more orders arrived from Sir George, instructing Rae to continue the search, as part of the major effort to find Franklin. His departure was regretted, for the Bay was well aware of his effectiveness. Robert Campbell, a senior Bay employee, wrote of Rae's 'known talent, probity and honour' and added, 'he is just the Spirit that would soon place the affairs of the District in a prosperous condition'.

Rae spent the winter in Fort Confidence, preparing for the expedition, and set out in April 1851. His account illustrates what Arctic travel was like, with spring approaching but conditions still difficult.

> We met with much rough ice on this nights journey and the walking was very bad near the shore, the snow being deep and soft. Shot a hare which was cooking in the kettle ten minutes afterwards. Sandpipers were seen and

some large flocks of Eider ducks flying eastward. On the night of the 31st [May], we crossed a low part of Cape Krusenstern and at 3.0am in the morning of the 1st June enjoyed the unusual luxury at that hour of having some tea being able to boil the kettle with some fuel found near Cape Lockyer, which I crossed over. The sledges going round. Some deer were seen, two of them large bucks whose horns were already nearly 2 feet long. A number of white owls were observed, one of which and a laughing goose, were shot by Beads. Both were put into the kettle and made an excellent supper. We could not easily decide whether the owl or the goose was best. They were both fat and well flavoured.

Fort Simpson on the Mackenzie River, 1852. Rae was based here in 1849. Pen and ink drawing by Alexander Hunter Murray.

By the end of June, with the ice breaking up, fish were being added to the diet. At Bloody Fall on the Coppermine salmon were netted and there was 'a general fish feast'.

This time Rae landed on Wollaston Peninsula and journeyed to the east and west with two men, two sledges and five dogs. It was hard going, a thaw making it necessary to take long detours 'to find a good road for the sledges' which were nevertheless 'much injured by the stones'. Deep ravines had to be crossed, and because of the fierce glare

from the sun it was necessary to travel by night. Rae shot whatever game he could, but the staple diet now was flour and pemmican.

Later in the season he was able to explore further by boat north and east up the coast of Victoria Island. Journeys inland were made on foot, but the ground was very rough, wearing out moccasins and lacerating the feet. There was no trace of Franklin, his ships or his men. It was only on the return journey when Rae found, in Parker Bay on the south coast of Victoria Island, two pieces of wood, which in his report he described but did not speculate on. It was later that he thought they were probably fragments of one of Franklin's vessels. The journey back to Fort Confidence involved a ten day battle up the Coppermine River in extremely hazardous conditions.

Again, Rae had to report negatively: 'My search for Franklin has been fruitless.' But in spite of this it had in many ways been a successful expedition, well-organized, disciplined and courageous in difficult and hostile circumstances, adding considerably to knowledge of the country and making the most of its resources. Although he had learned nothing of Franklin, he had most successfully put to the test his own techniques and practices for progress and survival in the Arctic.

This was formally acknowledged. In May 1852 Rae was awarded the Founder's Gold Medal of the Royal Geographical Society 'for his

survey of Boothia under most severe privations in 1848, and for his recent explorations on which very important additions have been made to the geography of the Arctic regions'. Although back in England, Rae was not in London for the presentation, but Sir Roderick Murchison, President of the Society, made reference to his 'boldness never surpassed' and his 'judgment and perseverance'. Describing his most recent journey, Murchison said, 'he set out accompanied by two men only, and trusting solely for shelter to snow-houses, which he taught his men to build, accomplished a distance of 1060 miles in 39 days...a feat which has never been equalled in Arctic travelling'.

Rae clearly valued this award, but there was another kind of recognition, not explicit but nevertheless embedded in Arctic tradition - the recognition by the Inuit of Rae's courage and ability. In Inuit eyes Rae stood out amongst the Europeans who traversed the Arctic regions. He may have been the legendary 'Aglooka', 'the one with long strides' (though he shares that possible attribution with James Clark Ross and Captain Crozier of the *Terror*). The Inuit trusted and respected him, probably as much because the respect was mutual as because of his Arctic aptitudes.

There remained gaps in the knowledge of the Arctic coastline and Rae was keen to continue his explorations in order to fill these. One of his purposes in England was to set up what would be his fourth and last

The Arctic in August. Looking north through Robeson Channel. Watercolour by Thomas Mitchell, a member of the Nares expedition, 1875. Arctic exploration continued after the 1850s, but Rae was critical of its elaborate extravagance.

Boothian Inuit drawn by John Ross, around 1835. Left to right: Alictu and Kanguagiu, Manellia and Adelik, Kunana. Rae encountered Inuit from the same area.

Arctic expedition. Its aims, approved by the Hudson's Bay Company, were entirely geographical - Rae himself said in a letter to *The Times* of 27 November 1852, 'I do not mention the lost navigators, as there is not the slightest hope of finding any traces of them in the quarter to which I am going.' In fact, it was this expedition that brought the first news of Franklin's fate.

Rae was back in North America in the summer of 1853, reaching York Factory in June and going on to Churchill and Repulse Bay, where they wintered. It was in the following spring that they met the Inuit who provided the first intimations of what had happened to Franklin. Rae continued his explorations as planned, west and north over uncharted territory, demonstrating that King William Island was indeed an island and confirming once and for all that Boothia was not. These missing pieces of the extraordinarily complex jigsaw of island, isthmus and strait that had defeated the north-west coast searchers were finally fitted together. Later, back in Repulse Bay, more Inuit confirmed the probability of the demise of the Franklin expedition through sickness and starvation.

Rae returned to England and was at once embroiled in controversy. In many ways, the arguments and hesitations about the value of Rae's information concerning Franklin highlighted the differences between the approaches and priorities of the Admiralty and the Hudson's Bay Company. There were both political and psychological undercurrents. The Company was very powerful, both commercially and in their understanding of the territory. The Royal Navy wanted the credit not only for heroic endeavour but also for success, and so must have been made uncomfortable by a scenario that suggested that there had been little of either attached to the Franklin expedition. The fact that the Franklin search had captured the popular imagination did not help.

The attitude of officialdom to the Hudson's Bay Company had always been grudging, with a marked reluctance to acknowledge their achievements in exploration. Little credence was given, for example, to the pioneering journeys of Bay employee Samuel Hearne in the 1770s, and similar establishment views seemed to linger in Rae's time. Nevertheless, it was impossible to ignore his extraordinary abilities and manifest achievements, even if there was little formal acknowledgement in Britain, beyond the financial reward which he eventually received.

Amongst the native North Americans and the pioneering incomers the view of Rae was rather different. The Inuit admired and respected him. They understood in a way no others could the nature of his acceptance of the Arctic and its people. He was hostile to neither, but had a tolerant and utilitarian openness to what both could offer. The Hudson's Bay Company also valued him highly, as tributes from Sir George Simpson, Robert Campbell and others indicated.

Rae's Arctic explorations were at an end, but not his North American travels. He left the service of the Hudson's Bay Company. For a while he was based in Hamilton, Ontario, where two of his brothers were, but it was hardly a sedentary existence. He thought nothing of walking the forty miles to Toronto for dinner. In 1860 he married Catherine Thompson, whose family was from County Tyrone in Ireland. In that same year Rae was employed to work on the Atlantic telegraph survey. He was in the Faroes, crossed Iceland on horseback, and then went on to Greenland, which extended his knowledge of the Inuit. In 1861 he took part in a hunting expedition which took him and a party of eleven up the North Saskatchewan River, through a number of unexplored areas and into the Rockies. Rae took the opportunity to carry

John Rae and his wife Catherine.

63

Rae in old age, showing a map of his travels and relics of the Franklin expedition.

Right: Relics of the Franklin expedition acquired by Rae and now in the National Museums of Scotland.

out surveying work, which added significantly to the geography of the North America. Three years later he was engaged to survey another telegraph route, from Red River to Vancouver Island, crossing the Rockies through the Yellowhead Pass. Although the construction of the telegraph itself was slow to follow, this, Rae's last North American journey, suggests an almost symbolic coda to his great years of exploration, engaged as he was in a task that inevitably encouraged cultivation and commerce to take hold in the wilderness.

With nearly three decades of his life in front of him, Rae returned to Britain. He lived for two years in Orkney, at Berstane House near Kirkwall, and was awarded an honorary degree by the University of Edinburgh. The citation described Rae's Arctic travels, and went on:

> On none of these occasions did Dr Rae allow any opportunity to escape of advancing our knowledge of the geography, meteorology and natural history of the far north-west and frozen regions, and it is not to be forgotten that he it was who first obtained definite information of the fate of Sir John Franklin and his gallant comrades...

Rae spent his remaining twenty-three years in London. He lectured, wrote scientific papers, and continued an active involvement in the Arctic, although he never returned. (He did visit Canada in 1882, and was in Montreal to present a paper on 'Arctic Exploration in North America' to the American Association for the Advancement of Science.) He wrote a great deal about travelling techniques in the Arctic and continued to argue the value of small-scale expeditions with experienced men equipped to live off the land, as against large-scale naval exploration, but officialdom was reluctant to listen to him. He regularly visited Orkney, and even in old age was recognizable as 'Rae of the Arctic', as an article in the Hudson's Bay Company's magazine *The Beaver* records:

> Those of us who saw him on his annual visits to Orkney even when he was close on his allotted span can never forget his striking figure, his indomitable expression, and how, shouldering his fowling piece, he strode along at a pace which left younger men far behind.

A later explorer, Dr Vilhjalmur Stefansson, paid tribute to Rae. He was, he said, 'a man exact and truthful, and in his methods of travel a generation ahead of his time'. But in some respects he was very much a man of his time and place, sharing the values of individualism and enterprise that were a feature of Victorian Scotland, and blending them with skills bred of a rugged background and enhanced by a determined and inbuilt independence. He himself identified these characteristics with the Hudson's Bay Company, but at the same time he clearly knew that he was remarkable, and his habit of understatement does not disguise this. He may have referred to Arctic travel as an 'ordinary journey' but it only takes a few words of his own accounts to belie that description.

RAE
AND THE
NATIVE CANADIANS

Dale Idiens

Although only twenty years old when he arrived in Canada, Dr John Rae's background and upbringing fitted him well for life in the Subarctic and Arctic. Orkney and Canada in the early nineteenth century had certain similarities, and like many of his countrymen Rae found his first experiences of Moose Factory, the Hudson's Bay Company fort on the south shore of Hudson Bay, so congenial that he stayed once his initial contract had expired.

Life in Orkney at the start of the nineteenth century was hard. Until agricultural improvements were introduced in the middle of the century Orkney farming was of the 'runrig' type, little patches of tillage among great stretches of moorland. Most people were subsistence farmers living in small stone-walled dwellings, with turf roofs weighted by stones. The houses were heated by open peat fires and in winter were shared with the farm animals. Technology and material life were generally simple, the need for domestic and working equipment being met from local materials such as wood, stone, bone, horn, leather, clay, straw and wool, with the addition of iron, cloth and other goods from outside. Fishing, fowling and hunting for small game were important activities, but nonetheless the people were poor and there was often famine.

The fact that the land could not support the population benefited not only Hudson's Bay Company recruitment, but also the whaling industry and the Navy. The Hudson's Bay Company was the least favoured option locally, regarded by many as dangerous and unpatriotic work. Nonetheless, it had attraction, since in the territory that in 1869 became Canada it was possible to earn twice the wage of an agricultural labourer in Orkney, and there was generally an adequate number of volunteers. In the late eighteenth and early nineteenth

Opposite: Cree Indians at York Factory. Detail from a watercolour by Peter Rindisbacher (1806-34).

centuries, when the population of Stromness, 'an irregular assemblage of dirty huts', was about two thousand souls, between sixty and a hundred Orcadians were engaged annually. At this period almost three-quarters of the Hudson's Bay Company staff in Canada were from Orkney.

Rae's youthful experience of the rigours of outdoor life encouraged his development into a hardy and resourceful individual with a passion for the sporting life. In this, however, he differed only in degree from many of the Orcadians who joined the Hudson's Bay Company, and other reasons must be sought to explain Rae's phenomenal success as an Arctic explorer.

A significant factor was temperament. Rae found in Canada that he preferred the company of Indian and Inuit hunting partners and Scots 'half-breeds' to 'the disagreeable people in Western life' he encountered as part of the white establishment. He explained:

> In using the term 'half-breed' I mean any of those who have Indian blood in their veins, in a greater or less degree, nor is this meant in the least as a term of reproach, for they are a very fine race, active, good looking, intelligent ... I especially refer to the English and Scotch half-breeds, with whom I am best acquainted, and who for travelling ... and for shooting and fishing companions I would prefer to any man I know, especially if mixed with a few experienced men from the Orkney Islands of Scotland, who for some duties are to be preferred.

This inclination may have been partly due to an egalitarian Scottish upbringing and education, but also had to do with Rae's natural admiration for those who excelled, as he did, in hunting, shooting, fishing and sailing. Such attitudes were not general among Europeans at the time and Rae was distrusted by many of his contemporaries for 'going native'.

Something of a perfectionist, Rae had a quick temper and was critical of anyone who failed to meet his own high standards, whether white or native Canadian. For example, when he was second in command to Sir John Richardson in 1848 on an Admiralty expedition in search of Franklin, whilst privately critical of Richardson and his methods, Rae was openly annoyed by the incompetence of the men

Orcadian (left) and Inuit netting birds. The technique is remarkably similar. *G H Robertson*, and (right) detail from a sketch by George Seton.

recruited by the Admiralty in England. They were mostly sappers and miners, with a few seamen, and had no experience of the Arctic, 'the most awkward, lazy and careless set I ever had anything to do with'. In his unpublished autobiography Rae returned to this point:

> It may seem very unnecessary and invidious to mention the fact, nor would I do so were it not that I have heard it stated over and over again that the men of our army and navy were as capable of doing portage work efficiently without being trained to it, as the experienced Hudson's Bay voyageur. I have never found it so.

However, Rae was also ready to praise skill and performance although his admiration of native ways was not always welcomed by others. Some Hudson's Bay Company colleagues felt he was over generous to the Indians. Robert Cowie, whom Rae was to have replaced at the Rupert River District in 1844 until Sir George Simpson decided to use Rae to complete the survey of the Arctic Coast, complained that Rae 'is over liberal in all payments to Indians'. When Rae brought news of the fate of the Franklin expedition to England in 1854, much of London society was astonished that Rae should have accepted the word of the Inuit without confirming the evidence for himself. Rae for his part believed that it was essential to 'communicate with as little loss of time as possible the melancholy tidings which I had heard, and thereby save the risk of more valuable lives being jeopardised'. He argued strongly for the veracity of the Inuit: 'I had good opportunities of putting this to the test... they did tell falsehoods occasionally, which might in some measure be justified, because they did so to endeavour to prevent us from travelling over their favourite hunting grounds.'

Although Rae's opinion of the native people was almost always high, there were exceptions. For example, in 1848 while preparing for the Franklin search expedition with Sir John Richardson, Rae said of an Iroquois guide, Thomas Karahouton, that he was 'sulky, lazy and soft and would have been insolent had he dared. We had three much better guides and more active men in the canoe than him vis Thos. Petit, Lazard Tacanajaze and Ignace Atawadkon.'

In both his published and his unpublished writings Rae recorded not only the names of his expedition companions, Indians, Inuit, Orcadians

Inside a Cree Indian tent, 1820, engraved after a drawing by Robin Hood.

and Scotsmen, but also the names of many of the native peoples he encountered on his journeys. In his published narrative of 1846-7 fourteen Inuit were individually named, while in his unpublished and incomplete autobiography he specifically referred to nineteen Indians and Inuit. Three of these were Inuit, Albert, William Ouligbuck and Munro; one was the Iroquois Baptiste Ra-ra-hoton; several were Dogrib Indians; while the majority were Cree 'half-breeds' (Métis) or, like George Rivers, Nibitabo and Thomas Mistegan, pure Cree Indians.

Inuit skinning caribou in the Repulse Bay area. Techniques have changed little since Rae's time.

During the first decade Rae spent in Canada at Moose Factory, George Rivers was a regular hunting companion and the two men became good friends, accustomed to spending days together on shooting expeditions, sleeping out under the same blankets and oilcloth. Rae found life at Moose Factory 'a wholly new one to me but I took to it very readily as there were ample means of gratifying some of my most cherished earlier pastimes, however in a totally different manner from what I had been accustomed to - so that I had much to learn!' It is clear that the Cree Indian George Rivers was an able mentor who made learning a pleasure for Rae:

> ...when Rivers was with me we lived most luxuriously as he brought his admirable cooking qualities to the marsh, and the ducks, geese or godwits when either boiled or fried by him were very different articles of diet from the same food when cooked by myself.

Rae added, 'George was a first rate and fearless canoe man and an admirable shot, I also after very considerable practice became fairly good.' Perhaps as an acknowledgment of the value of his practice with Rivers, Rae satisfied his friend's 'great ambition of getting a double barrel by ordering him a very powerful one from England with which he made wonderfully long shots'.

George may have failed to teach John Rae how to be a good cook, but he and other native companions certainly introduced Rae to new techniques of hunting and trapping, passing on their knowledge of the many species of game and fish, which were different from those he had been accustomed to in Orkney. Rae also learned aboriginal techniques of cleaning, skinning and butchering large game such as caribou, securing the blood in a bag formed by the stomach turned inside out, or if time was short at least removing the gullet, since, 'were this not done, the meat would in a few hours go tainted as to be scarcely fit for food'. When hunting to feed his expedition party Rae learned to 'cache' each kill under a heap of heavy stones to protect it from predators such as wolves and wolverines, until he or his men could return to collect it. If possible, wounded animals were made to walk as near to the hunter's sledge as possible before finally being despatched, to save effort and energy.

The Barren Grounds, with stone ambush used when hunting caribou. *Fred Bruemmer*

Ouligbuck, a member of Franklin's 1825 expedition and of Rae's first expedition. Detail from a drawing by George Back.

At Repulse Bay in 1853 Rae's party spent the autumn laying up stocks of fuel and food for the severe winter ahead. Game was scarce and Rae detailed the efforts needed by everyone to lay in sufficient provisions to ensure their survival. In one day's hunting Rae describes how he walked or ran more than thirty miles, shot, skinned and butchered five deer, carried some of them a considerable distance and gathered together four or five tons of stones to make the caches. For a day's hunting trip his equipment was 'simple enough, consisting of a very heavy double rifle, powder flask and bullet pouch, large clasp knife and spring catch, bag for small game, deer tongues and other delicacies - also a carrying strap in which I usually carried home a fairish load'. He lists the total quantity of game killed at Repulse Bay in September 1853 as ninety-six deer, one hare, one seal, ninety-six ptarmigan, fifty-one salmon and three trout. 'Of the deer 40 were shot by myself, 18 by our hunter Mistegan, 13 by Jacob Beads, 9 by Ouligbuck, 5 by Johnstone, 3 by John Beads, and 4 each by McDonald and McLellan.'

Another Cree Indian, Nibitabo, was chosen by Rae to accompany his first expedition to the Arctic in 1846-7. The party succeeded in wintering at Repulse Bay, enduring severe temperatures that reached -47° and critical food shortages. Despite his resourcefulness Rae was very dependent upon his native companions. He described Nibitabo as 'one of the keenest sportsmen I have ever met with', and employed him again on the 1848 expedition with Sir John Richardson. The local Inuit encountered at Repulse Bay also provided much support. Rae referred to several of them, including I-vit-Chuck, who was 'always willing and obedient, and generally lively and cheerful except when very tired. He accommodates himself easily to our manners and customs.'

Rae employed two Inuit hunters and interpreters on his first Arctic expedition in 1846. Ouligbuck, who had accompanied Sir John Franklin's early expeditions and those of Sir John Richardson, and his son William. Rae set a fierce pace on his two overland marches to explore Pelly Bay and the west coast of Melville Peninsula in 1846 and 1847, and himself admitted to severe fatigue. William Ouligbuck became so exhausted he was sent back to base camp at Repulse Bay. Rae admired old Ouligbuck - 'as brave a man as I ever met' - but had mixed views about William - 'one of the greatest rascals unhung' -

Bloody Fall on the Coppermine River, 1821, where one of Rae's men was drowned - the only fatality in any of his expeditions. Engraved after a drawing by George Back.

and for his final exploring expedition in 1853-4 would have preferred the younger brother Donald Ouligbuck. Nonetheless, Rae acknowledged William's skills as an interpreter - 'in addition to his own language he spoke English, Cree, and French passably well' - and ensured that William received his share, £210, of the British Government's reward for news of the Franklin expedition.

Rae had a high opinion of two other Inuit companions. Albert, or Albert One-Eye, was engaged as interpreter with Sir John Richardson's 1848 expedition. Albert came from Eastmain, or the east shore of Hudson Bay, yet he had no difficulty in making himself understood by Inuit encountered on the Mackenzie River by Richardson and Rae. The following spring Albert accompanied Rae down the Coppermine River in a further attempt to reach Wollaston Peninsula. This failed again because of the ice and on the return journey Albert was accidentally drowned at Bloody Fall. He was the only fatality on any of Rae's expeditions, and Rae felt the loss keenly: 'Albert was liked by everyone, for his good humour, lively disposition and great activity... I had become much attached to the poor fellow ...'

On Rae's fourth and final expedition to Repulse Bay in 1853, Munro, an Inuit from Churchill was engaged as interpreter, together with William Ouligbuck. The expedition boats stopped south of Knapp's Bay to enable Munro to say farewell to his family. Rae noted that when he came back to the boats 'he looked in very low spirits' and learned from his men that 'the parting of the poor fellow with his wife and children had been most tender and affectionate'. Soon Rae discovered that Munro was little use as an interpreter, although 'a very good lad' and at Chesterfield Inlet he was sent home. This last expedition also included in the party Thomas Mistegan, a Cree Indian from Norway House. Rae remarked upon Mistegan's 'great intelligence and activity' and describes him as 'a very able man and expert sledge hauler'. Mistegan was an exceptional shot and Rae recorded with admiration numerous examples of his skills, including one occasion when Mistegan killed 'two fine fat bucks' with one shot. 'He waited until they were in line, then sent a ball through both.'

When travelling further west in the vicinity of the Coppermine and Mackenzie Rivers Rae came into contact with Athapaskan or Dene Indians, including Dogrib, whose skills and techniques he also praised. In September 1848, for example, when returning with Sir John Richardson to Fort Confidence on Great Bear Lake, they took a guide from a Dogrib encampment:

> We found our Indian companion a very great use, as he, although apparently taking us by very roundabout and crooked ways, always chose almost intuitively the best route. It was even an advantage to walk next to him, for by putting the foot exactly where he had put his, gave the surest support.

Rae enjoyed the company of Indians and Inuit and learned well from them although there were occasions when he regretted his failure to take good advice. Of Baptiste Ra-ra hoton, an Iroquois Indian, Rae wrote, 'One of the best and bravest canoe men, I ever saw, at the same time very prudent', and went on to describe an incident on Lake Superior when Rae insisted upon embarking upon the lake in a canoe against the advice of Baptiste, putting both of them at risk: 'He behaved

Opposite: Migrating caribou. The movements of animals provided clues as to weather and seasonal changes. *Fred Bruemmer*

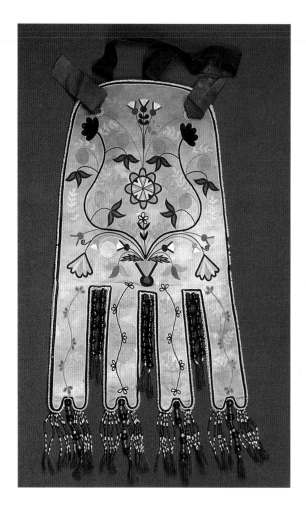

Rae's 'octopus' bag. Rae designed
patterns for beadwork and embroidery.
This pattern may have been one of his own
designs.

like a trump however and... brought the canoe to harbour having taken
us through a sea, which under less able management would probably
have swallowed us.' It was rare for Rae to admit a mistake, but on this
and other occasions he gave full credit to his native companion.

Rae had considerable admiration for the skills of native women and
frequently commented upon their abilities. He had respect for Cree
Indian women:

> ...they manage a small canoe skilfully, and by setting nets...add very much
> to the comfort and variety of their diet... In winter and spring they angle
> successfully for trout through holes cut in the ice, set snares for ...
> hares...and some of them shoot not badly.

At Repulse Bay in July 1847 Rae described Inuit methods of seal hunting on the ice. Some Inuit could mimic the movements of the seal so
well that the animal was actually encouraged to leave its ice hole and
move towards the hunter: 'Women are very expert at this and frequently have no spear using only a small club of wood to strike the
seal on the nose.' A map drawn for Edward Parry of the west side of
Melville Peninsula by an Inuit woman at Igloolik in 1821 was later
found by Rae 'to be made fully accurate'.

Rae also appreciated the skill and workmanship of Indian women in
decorating dress and accessories for themselves and their families. In
1860 he was painted in watercolours wearing skin clothing with deco-
rated accessories of Cree style. Rae's own collection includes a set of
similar items, a belt, pair of garters, two bags and a gun cover, all made
of moose or caribou skin and beautifully ornamented with porcupine
quillwork, moosehair or European embroidery silk. Since Rae records
in his autobiography that he turned his hand to designing patterns for
bead and silkwork for the Indian women, it may be that the patterns,
for example on the 'octopus' bag which appears to be embroidered
with thistles, were designed by Rae himself, and the finished articles
commissioned from a Cree craftswoman.

Rae's enthusiasm for native skills and techniques went beyond pas-
sive observation. He was an eager pupil who put into practice much of
what he learned from his Indian and Inuit companions. Rae's adoption
of, for example, the Indian-style low, flat sledge with flexible runners,

Snowshoeing Indians, wearing Hudson's Bay Company blankets, and using the flat style sledges favoured by Rae. Watercolour by Dennis Gale.

Inuit women of Igloolik, engraved from a drawing by Capt. Lyon, 1821.

snowshoes and Inuit snow houses contributed greatly to his success at a period when many official expeditions chose to underestimate or ignore local knowledge. Snowshoes are a classic example.

> At first I could not be persuaded that a person could walk better with such great clumsy looking things as snowshoes on his feet crunching knee deep in snow, but it did not require very long practice to decide this question in favour of the snowshoes.

Soon he became an expert.

> Of snowshoes there are five or six different shapes, which are worn according to the taste and custom of the wearer, or according to the sort of snow he has to walk on in the woods or in the open. In the woods for instance where the snow is usually compact, and into which the snowshoe sinks deep, the flat snowshoe is the best, the favourite size and shape was nearly 4 feet long x 1 foot or more broad, the size depending of course, much upon the weight of the wearer. After some time I made my own, which were very light, the frames being of the usual menache, tough birchwood, the netting work is usually performed by the women, some of whom are very expert and do this work with great neatness.

Rae understood the technology of the snowshoe.

> A properly constructed snowshoe should be so balanced that its forepart only should be lifted off the snow where the foot is raised, and it may be considered a fair proportion of this distribution of weight, if a snowshoe of two and a quarter pounds has so much of its weight round the tailpart resting on the snow, that the weight raised by the foot at each end is only one and a half pounds, that is, it should loose one fourth of its weight. The great mistake in the construction of snowshoes even by experienced persons is often made, in not giving sufficient extent of surface in the forepart. If this is not done although the shoe balances well enough when lifted, it goes down deeper in the snow forward than at the aft part, causing much useless labour and discomfort.

Rae regarded walking on snowshoes as 'one of the finest exercises in the world for strengthening the limbs' and made his own snowshoes, netting them himself, although generally this was a woman's task.

Rae was not the first white explorer in Canada to adopt native ways, for Hudson's Bay Company men already practised a number of local

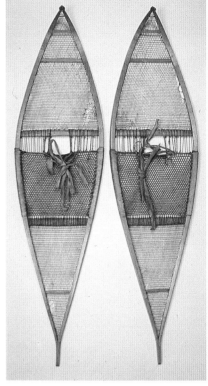

Above: Snowshoes used by John Rae.

Above left: Dogrib Indian making a snowshoe frame, Fort Rae, North West Territory, 1937. *A Keefer*

Left: Dogrib Indian woman threading a snowshoe frame, Mackenzie River, 1920.

John Rae's moccasins.

methods. But Rae was the best and the most successful. Sir George Simpson, Overseas Governor of the Hudson's Bay Company, wanted to complete the survey of the remaining unmapped sections of the Arctic Coast on behalf of the Company and he found in Rae someone with the physical stamina, the inclination and the skill to live off the land, travel light and overwinter in the Arctic like the native peoples. Simpson wrote to Rae in 1844, 'As regards the management of people and endurance of toil, either in walking, boating or starving, I think you are better adapted for this work than most of the gentlemen with whom I am acquainted.' It was these abilities, based on Rae's personal qualities and improved by his experience of aboriginal methods, that enabled Rae to travel further, faster, and cover more Arctic miles than any previous white explorer. The part that Rae's Indian and Inuit companions and instructors played in this achievement was crucial and merits recognition.

Rae aimed for his expeditions to travel light.

> Our dresses like our bedding were extremely light as compared with those of the Government Arctic Expeditions, which must have been not only a great encumbrance when walking, but have caused as we are told they did, a great amount of perspiration which by freezing on the woollens, caused no little discomfort!

He described his own dress in the winter of 1853 at Repulse Bay as 'neither so heavy nor so warm looking as the dress is very commonly used on a cold winter's day in England'. It consisted of a fur cap, large leather mitts with fur at the wrist lined with thick blanket, smoked mooseskin moccasins, with two or three blanket socks, and thongs of skin stitched on the soles to prevent them slipping, light cloth coat, the hood and sleeves lined with chamois leather, a cloth vest, and pair of thin mooseskin trousers. In extremely cold weather Rae and his men traded with the Inuit for caribou skin clothing, and his accounts regularly refer to the acquisition of waterproof sealskin boots from the Inuit.

The winter of 1846-7 was the first time a European-led party had succeeded in overwintering in the Arctic by living off the land. Earlier expeditions had only managed to do so by carrying massive quantities of supplies with them, very difficult without a ship. Rae's party of twelve set off in 1846 with sufficient provisions for only four months, yet they expected to be away for at least a year. In the event this expedition took fifteen months. A crack shot himself, and a prodigious hunter, Rae ensured that he and his men had fresh meat whenever possible.

Although on occasion Rae used dogs to haul sledges on his expeditions, generally he and his party pulled their own loads on flat Indian-style sledges. The men had loads weighing about seventy pounds each, while Rae's own sledge was usually lighter, at around forty pounds, enabling him to undertake the necessary measurements for mapping. Rae's sleeping gear weighed no more than five pounds compared with almost twenty-five pounds of bedding per man carried by other expeditions at this time. In 1853 at Repulse Bay, preparing to journey northward, Rae said of his party:

> Our total bedding consisted of a blanket and a half stitched together and five strips of deerskin with the hair on, the lightest we could find to place between us and the snow. The whole of this bedding for five persons weighed less than 25lbs.

As the weather cooled at night the men slept together under shared blankets for warmth. Rae compared the practices of official government expeditions unfavourably with his own and described how his expedition's sleeping arrangements worked:

> There were five of us, and we all lay under one covering taking our coats off so that our arms might be more closely in contact, our moccasins was all the undressing we went through. I *always* occupied an outside place, and the cook to be for the next day the other. Those inside were warm enough, but when either of the outsiders felt chilly on the exposed side, all he had to do was to turn round, give his neighbour a nudge and we all put about, and the chilly party was soon warmed. We got so speedily accustomed to this, that I believe we used to move over from one side to the other when required without wakening.

During the expedition season, once the weather became good enough to travel in the Arctic, it quickly became too hot in the middle of the day for walking, so the party would rest or sleep in daylight and march at night, starting at 7 or 8pm in the evening and stopping at 3 or 4am.

However, by May even walking at night was less than pleasant as the temperature at midnight could reach 22°. Unencumbered by unsuitable clothing and excessive supplies, Rae was able to move fast, taking full advantage of the short travelling season in the Arctic.

In his account for 2 May 1851, travelling with two Red River Métis, Beads and Linklater, Rae describes their method of travelling as

> ...different from that of the Government sledging parties in various ways. But especially in not stopping to take lunch or dinner... A mouthful of pemmican carried in the pocket or placed conveniently on the sledges served to keep away hunger sufficiently until supper time. For myself I was wholly independent of my companions having my bedding, instruments, gun and a good supply of pemmican on my sledge with the requisite tools for building a snow hut if required. I could thus examine bays, rivers, inlets and other localities on the route when requisite, whilst my men were making a straight course.

Rae's equipment was minimal. In addition to Inuit snowgoggles, which he regarded as perfect of their kind, tools for building a snow house and a small supply of provisions - these consisted of his gun, watch, octant, chronometers, telescope and needlecase. He also carried a few books, including a volume of Shakespeare and one of sacred poetry (his favourite poem was 'The Power of God'). When the books froze Rae took them to bed with him to thaw out the pages.

For his first winter in the Arctic at Repulse Bay in 1846-7 Rae's party constructed a stone house, Fort Hope. It took a month to build and despite two-feet thick walls, proved to be very uncomfortable. Because of a fuel shortage Rae and his men were 'lying occasionally 14 hours in bed, as to sit up in a house in below zero temperatures without light or fire was not very pleasant'. Indeed it was not until March 1847 that Rae was able to dry his blankets in the sun, the first time in three months that they had been free of ice, and he habitually ran 'smartly up and down of a night' on rocks, to warm his feet before going to bed. As a consequence Rae quickly recognized the advantages of the Inuit snowhouses and learned to build one himself. 'I attempted to build a snowhouse after the native fashion and succeeded tolerably well - after a few trials one or two of the men became very good masons.'

Building a snowhouse drawn by W Klutschak, 1879. Schwatka's expedition, of which Klutschak was a member, like Rae adopted native survival techniques.

Opposite: Personal items belonging to Rae - Volume of Shakespeare's plays, book of poetry, needlecase and watch.

85

Rae realized that not only the construction of the snowhouse but its siting was of importance when he observed that the Inuit built their snow houses in a more sheltered position than his own. 'This would have been the best situation for our establishment...but we were too late in making the discovery.' When he returned to Repulse Bay several years later, in 1854, Rae remembered this and the party built their snow houses 'on the SES side of Beacon Hill, by which they were all protected from the prevailing NW gales'. Fort Hope was not occupied. Rae urged the advantages of snowhouses over other forms of shelter especially tents.

> The advantages of the snowhut are manifold. It does away with the requiring of nearly so much bedding. The moisture from the breath and from the warm food adheres to the wall. In the most stormy weather it is impenetrable by wind and although it takes on average an hour to build, it remains ready, if the door is blocked up with snow, for your return journey.

Rae's resentment at the failure of the British Government and Admiralty to take his advice regarding the adoption of native techniques on official Arctic expeditions, especially snowshoes, sledges and snowhouses, continued all his life. He described the Nares expedition of 1875 as an 'extravagantly equipped expedition that showed ludicrous stupidity and ignorance', and never failed to castigate the Establishment on this score, writing letters to the press and publishing articles.

However, mid-nineteenth-century Britain did produce one item of technology that Rae endorsed wholeheartedly, and next to his gun, octant, chronometer and watch was one of the few items of western equipment he was to insist upon for his expeditions. This was the Halkett India-rubber cloth boat.

The cloth boat, also sometimes called an air boat, invented in 1844 by Lieutenant Peter Halkett RN, was one of the earliest successful inflatable craft. The inventor's father, John Halkett, was a Director of the Hudson's Bay Company, so perhaps it was no accident that this light, portable boat was used so often by Rae and other explorers in the Arctic. It was made of layers of cotton fabric covered with rubber, and provided with brass nozzles for inflation and padded canvas fenders filled with cork. Once inflated, the cloth boat measured approximately

Above: Portage on the Trout River, 1820-1. First Franklin expedition, overland. Watercolour by Robert Hood.

Left: The crew of HMS *Terror* breaking a passage through the ice, Back's expedition of 1836-38: this contrasts strikingly with the very small numbers of men forming land-based expeditions and accompanying Rae. Engraved after a drawing by George Back.

9 by 4 feet and could carry two men or a substantial load. Deflated, it folded up into a back pack and was easily carried.

Rae used a Halkett cloth boat provided by Sir George Simpson on his first expedition in 1846-7. 'We had one of Halkett's air boats, large enough to carry three persons. This last useful and light little vessel ought to form part of the equipment of every expedition.' This expedition also had two wooden boats measuring twenty-two feet and seven feet six inches long respectively. From childhood, Rae had a great fondness for boats and used them on all his expeditions, sometimes designing and helping to build them himself. However, the larger wooden ones were difficult to portage between waterways, hence his enthusiasm for the Halkett inflatable. On the 1846 expedition it was used largely for setting and examining fishing nets.

The cloth boat was also suitable for transporting the expedition and its equipment across waterways. In September 1848, when accompanying

Sussex Lake engraved after a drawing by George Back, 1836. Scenes of this kind were familiar to Rae.

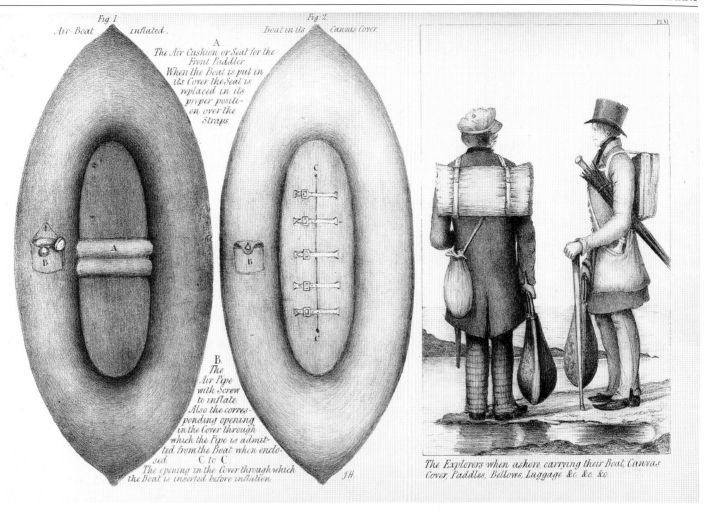

Fig.1

Air-Boat inflated.

Fig.2

Boat in its Canvas Cover.

Pl.VI

A.
The Air Cushion or Seat for the Front Paddler. When the Boat is put in its Cover the Seat is replaced in its proper position over the Straps.

B.
The Air Pipe with Screw to inflate. Also the corresponding opening in the Cover through which the Pipe is admitted from the Boat when enclosed.

C to C
The opening in the Cover through which the Boat is inserted before inflation.

J.H.

The Explorers when ashore carrying their Boat, Canvas-Cover, Paddles, Bellows, Luggage &c. &c. &c.

Illustrations of the inflatable boat designed by Lt Peter Halkett, taken from the London sales catalogue. Rae found the Halkett boat invaluable.

89

Sir John Richardson, Rae describes the crossing of Richardson River under somewhat unusual circumstances.

> A fire was lit so as to soften it [the Halkett boat] for the purpose of getting it more perfectly distended with air and I crossed over alone using two tin plates as paddles...the line that had been brought over was found to be too short for its purpose of hauling the boat backwards and forwards across the stream, but at the suggestion of Sir John, the portage or carrying straps were added. Albert, who came across next, was barely able to reach the shore, his hands having become quite powerless with cold when using the plate paddles. The real paddles had been left behind by the man of whose load they formed a part, the total weight not being more than 2 or 3 pounds!... The narrowest bits of the stream measured was about 110 yards, and the line being now long enough for the purpose, the party was soon ferried over at 14 trips...

This exercise took four hours. Because of the onset of winter the water ways began to freeze over, so the Halkett boat could no longer be used, and was left secured on a hill top with a marker. The following July Rae was fortunate enough to find the Halkett where it had been left, and it was used again.

For his final expedition in 1853 to complete the survey of Boothia for the Hudson's Bay Company Rae, who already had two Halkett boats for use on the expedition, requested a third from London, but this failed to appear.

> A beautiful Halkett boat was most generously presented to the expedition by the special friend of all Arctic explorers, John Barrow Esq. But unfortunately it got astray somewhere either en route to Liverpool or America and I never saw it until many years afterwards, when it had become deteriorated by damp.

This Halkett boat is probably the one which has survived intact on Orkney, the only example of this rare early inflatable known to exist. Painted on the bow are the words 'Dr. Rae, Hudson Bay', and on the stern 'James Fitzjames' (Fitzjames was commander of HMS *Erebus* on the lost Franklin expedition). Rae gave the boat to a friend in Orkney, and it is now in the care of the Stromness Natural History Society Museum Trust, Stromness.

Opposite: Late November freeze-up in Hudson Bay. The Bay has changed little since Rae's time. *Fred Bruemmer*

RAE
AS COLLECTOR
AND ETHNOGRAPHER

Dale Idiens

Rae's adoption of native Canadian methods was not random or accidental but deliberate and studied. He recorded Indian and Inuit techniques, collected examples of their ethnography or material culture and learned to use native methods and make native-style artefacts himself. Well over 200 Canadian Indian and Inuit artefacts collected by Rae are preserved in museums in Britain. These are in addition to the Franklin relics which Rae obtained from the Inuit at Repulse Bay in 1854 and brought back to London as evidence of the fate of the expedition, and the personal belongings he carried on his explorations, such as his watch, books, octant, snowshoes and moccasins which also survive.

His collection of aboriginal material culture is particularly remarkable given the difficulties of Arctic travel and Rae's efforts to travel light. In the eighteenth and early nineteenth centuries it was unusual for Arctic explorers to collect native artefacts at all. Maritime exploration using ships made the collection of 'curiosities' or man-made artefacts somewhat easier. Official naval voyages to the Arctic in the early nineteenth century, such as those of Ross, Parry and Beechey, often collected objects from native peoples they encountered, and many of these survive today in museums. But serious interest in ethnography was not widespread, although it had been common practice for many years to record unknown zoological and geological material in case of possible commercial exploitation. Such observations were frequently published as appendices to exploration accounts, and Rae himself conformed to this practice.

But Rae was part of a new attitude towards native artefacts which was beginning to become apparent by the mid-nineteenth century. An

Opposite: Haida Indian rattle from Nootka Sound, Vancouver Island, collected by Rae.

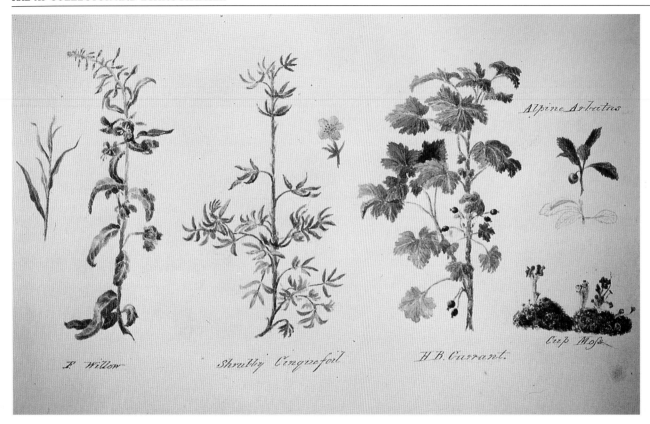

Above: Botanical sketches by George Back, 1825-6, of plants from the Mackenzie River area.

Right: Roseate or Ross's gull. Type specimens like this one, shot by James Clark Ross and now in the National Museums of Scotland, were brought back to Scotland for scientific collections.

important influence, not only upon Rae, but on a number of earlier Arctic explorers was Robert Jameson, Professor of Natural History at the University of Edinburgh between 1804 and 1854. A remarkable individual, Jameson was responsible for expanding the Natural History Museum of the University of Edinburgh, raising it to a position of pre-eminence in Britain and Europe. For fifty years Jameson inspired generations of students who attended his lectures on zoology. He took advantage of the fact that many graduates left Scotland to work abroad as a means of developing his museum collections, and in 1807, with royal approval, he issued printed collecting instructions to government departments in London, including the Admiralty.

Published in 1817, these instructions listed desired acquisitions for the museum in Edinburgh under zoological headings - Quadrupeds and Birds; Reptiles and Fish; Shells; Insects - and explained how to prepare, pack and transport such items. Jameson also included a section headed 'Antiquities, Articles of Dress, Agricultural, Hunting and Warlike Instruments etc of different Nations and Tribes', urging that 'the collecting of the various articles just enumerated, is particularly recommended, as these objects illustrate, in a very interesting manner, the past and present condition of the human species'. As a result of Jameson's efforts, collections of Arctic natural history, geology and ethnography, made by such individuals as Ross, Richardson, Franklin, Beechey and Parry, arrived in Edinburgh.

Natural history was not a compulsory subject for medical students but many of them did attend Jameson's lectures. For example, John Richardson while at Edinburgh University was taught by Robert Jameson. Although there is no firm evidence that Rae himself heard Jameson or visited the University museum during his years as a student in Edinburgh from 1829 to 1833, it is highly probable that he did so, and that he knew of Jameson's published collecting instructions which were issued to potential collectors.

The proposition that ethnographic artefacts, in addition to zoological and geological material, were worthy of collection had been part of the academic atmosphere in Edinburgh while Rae was there, an attitude which also received support from Sir George Simpson, Overseas Governor of the Hudson's Bay Company. When Rae received his official

Arctic fox, engraved from a drawing by John Ross.

orders for his first exploring expedition from Simpson in 1846, part of Simpson's letter stated:

> ...you will do your utmost, consistently with the success of your main object, to attend to botany and geology; to zoology in all its departments ... You will also, to the best of your opportunities, observe the ethnographical peculiarities of the Esquimaux of the country ... The particulars ... you will record fully and precisely in a journal, to be kept, as far as practicable, from day to day, collecting at the same time any new, curious or interesting specimens in illustration of any of the foregoing heads.

A significant factor in the development of new ideas regarding ethnography, especially the ethnography of non-European societies, was the Great Exhibition of 1851, which exhibited in the Crystal Palace, London, the artefacts of both industrialized and non-industrialized nations from all over the world. As a result, several influential individuals began to take an interest in the history of technology within the context of the evolution of culture. These included George Wilson, who in 1855 took up the first chair in technology at the University of Edinburgh and became first director of the Industrial Museum of Scotland (absorbing the collections of Jameson's Natural History Museum), and George Wilson's brother, Daniel Wilson, who was appointed to a chair at the University of Toronto in 1853. Within the wider framework of explaining the evolution of civilization, Daniel Wilson regarded the New World as the perfect testing ground in which a study of the Red Man 'still in a state of nature', could help explain the sequence of prehistoric man in the Old World. Daniel Wilson was to develop an intense interest in Canadian ethnography and in 1875 published his massive work, *Prehistoric Man,* in which he demonstrated a wideranging comparative knowledge not only of Canadian Indians, but of South American peoples, African tribes and Pacific Islanders. The Wilson brothers, with support from Sir George Simpson, initiated in 1857 the collecting of native Canadian material culture by Scots working in Hudson's Bay Company forts throughout north-west Canada. As a result, between 1858 and 1862, almost 300 Subarctic Indian artefacts and a considerable quantity of Inuit objects were sent to Edinburgh. This material, which was collected in response to a specific request, part of a defined museum collecting policy, resulted in one of the earliest systematic documented collections of ethnology from the interior of North America.

At the time, George and Daniel Wilson regarded their collecting activities as 'scientific'. Their aim was to collect within defined classifications and to exhibit in systematic arrangements. George Wilson prepared a list of specific collecting instructions which were circulated through Simpson in 1857 for issue to potential collectors. Written almost fifty years later than the instructions of Robert Jameson, Wilson's were organized differently, according to raw materials, tools, processes and finished products. They laid particular emphasis on the importance of recording and collecting the actual raw materials and tools used in the manufacturing processes, as well as collecting examples of the finished products. The focus was on industrial, or man-made, artefacts, and reflected Wilson's particular interest in technology.

In England, General Pitt Rivers, who had reorganized the British Museum's collection of Natural and Artificial Curiosities as an 'Ethnological Gallery' in 1845, was also developing theories regarding the classification of artefacts which he expounded in his writings and his own museum in the 1870s and 1880s. Like the Wilson brothers, Pitt Rivers aimed to instruct in the development of technology, using ordinary and typical specimens rather than rare objects, which had been selected and arranged in sequence. These academics and antiquarians, together with colleagues in Britain and Europe, were part of a new attitude towards the ethnography of peoples in other parts of the world, no longer regarding their material culture as 'curiosities', but as a potentially rewarding subject for systematic study.

Rae collected his Indian and Inuit material in the Canadian Arctic and Subarctic between 1846 and 1854, before most of these developments. However, while a student in Edinburgh Rae had been exposed to the emerging recognition of the importance of non-European ethnography in the early nineteenth century, views which were in turn endorsed by his superior Sir George Simpson. These attitudes, combined with Rae's own admiration for native Canadian technology and a practical desire to understand and utilize its methods, inspired him

Daniel Wilson, instrumental in arranging for Hudson's Bay Company employees to collect ethnographic and natural history material. Detail from an oil painting by Sir George Reid, 1891.

97

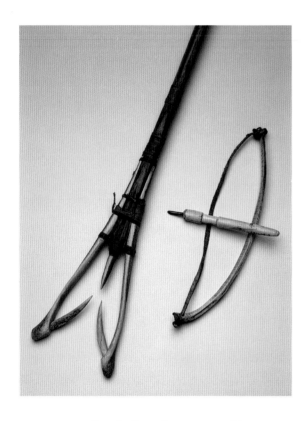

Repulse Bay salmon spear and iron-tipped bow-drill from Rankin's Inlet, collected by Rae.

to collect artefacts, despite the severe restraints imposed by overland travel in the Arctic.

When Rae retired from the Hudson's Bay Company in 1856, he returned to London where he was to base himself for the rest of his life, despite several working trips to Canada and many lengthy visits to Orkney. In London he joined a number of learned societies, including the Royal Geographical Society, where he would have encountered fellow member General Pitt Rivers. Having friends in Edinburgh, Rae could have met George Wilson before his premature death in 1859, and may well have visited the Industrial Museum of Scotland. It is quite possible that either before leaving Canada or on a subsequent visit he was introduced to Daniel Wilson through Sir George Simpson. Whether Rae knew such individuals personally is a matter for conjecture. But certainly his experience and interests were in tune with the new approaches to ethnography and anthropology which were emerging in the second half of the nineteenth century and Rae was one of a number of Scots who contributed to the early development of interest in native Canadian ethnography.

Rae's collection of artefacts, some of which he retained (a proportion was handed over to his official sponsors, the Hudson's Bay Company and the Admiralty) is important today for several reasons. A number of pieces are valuable because they can be identified with some confidence to particular places and times by reference to Rae's records. In July 1847 at Repulse Bay Rae described in great detail an Inuit salmon spear or leister:

> The spear is usually made of two diverging pieces of musk ox horn, from 4-5 inches apart at the extremities; between these there is a bone about 3-4 inches shorter than the other one. Each of the longer prongs is furnished with a bar on its inner side, made of a bent nail, or piece of bone, which prevents the fish from escaping. The handle is 6-8ft long.

He also explained the way in which the Inuit used such spears, by building a stone dam across a creek below the high water mark, to cut the salmon off from the sea at the ebb of the tide so that they could be more easily speared. A salmon spear which meets the above description (except that the handle has been cut down by about two feet,

Present-day Inuit fishing at Repulse Bay.
Fred Bruemmer

probably in order to ease transportation) and documented as coming from Repulse Bay is in Rae's collection.

On several subsequent occasions Rae was to reflect upon the usefulness of the salmon spears used by the Inuit at Repulse Bay. In August 1848 while travelling with Sir John Richardson he complained 'had we carried with us a spear similar to that used at Repulse Bay we might have speared a good many [salmon] - we could not take them with nets as we had neither depth nor extent of water'. A few months later in April 1849 while at Fort Confidence, Great Bear Lake, the local Indians were finding it so hard to obtain food that Rae, 'to show them that fish could be obtained without difficulty... made a small spear after the Eskimo fashion and in about an hour speared 70 herrings through a hole in the ice'.

Returning to Churchill on completing his first exploring expedition, Rae records in August 1847 picking up an Inuit ivory snowknife, a fire drill and an iron drill, at Rankin's Inlet on the west shore of the Hudson's Bay.

On Rae's second exploring expedition with Sir John Richardson, on returning to Fort Confidence in September 1848, he described the help given by a group of Copper Inuit to the exploration party in crossing

Copper Inuit knife from Rae River, and Copper Inuit arrowheads from Cape Flinders or Stromness Bay, collected by Rae.

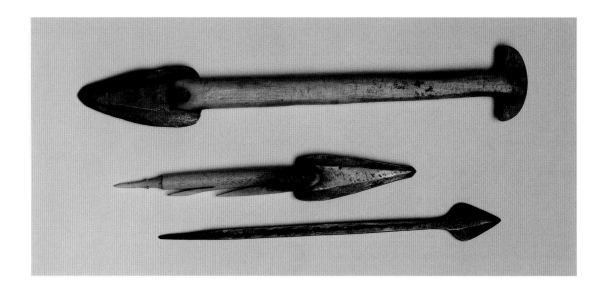

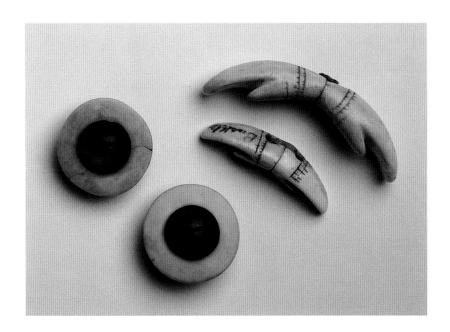

Inuit lip ornaments and ivory toggles in the form of mittens from the Mackenzie River area, collected by Rae.

Rae River. 'We paid them as well as we were able, yet for every article given they offered something in return, and I got a copper knife and dagger which I have brought on here.'

Earlier in 1848 Rae also collected a number of Mackenzie Inuit artefacts from natives encountered near the mouth of the Mackenzie River in the early stages of his expedition with Sir John Richardson. These included a snowknife, harpoon heads, stone net sinkers, men's lip ornaments or labrets and ivory toggles. Some of the objects, obtained from remote Inuit groups on the central Arctic coast which had no previous direct contact with white men, are effectively 'type' specimens for the study of traditional Inuit material culture.

In the summer of 1851 the Copper Inuit, whom Rae encountered off Cape Flinders and Stromness Bay on his third exploring expedition, told him they had never met white men before. Rae remarked on their 'spears, copper knives and bows and arrows (the latter pointed with bone, stone or copper)'. Rae's party traded meat with the Inuit for waterproof sealskin boots and it seems likely that other Copper Inuit

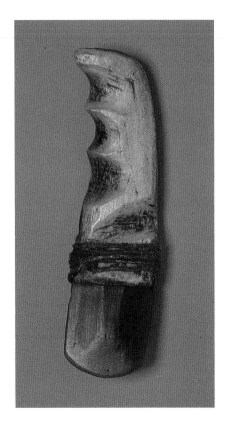

Woman's knife from Victoria Island, collected by Rae.

items in Rae's collection date to this exchange. This expedition was highly successful. In two journeys during a single season, one by foot and the other by boat, Rae finally succeeded in reaching Wollaston Peninsula and Victoria Island where he collected some rare dated and documented objects, including fire-making equipment and a woman's knife with a nephrite blade.

A number of items in the collection cannot be dated nor located precisely, although they are most likely to have been collected by Rae on one of his four expeditions between 1846 and 1854. These include harpoon heads, spear and arrowheads, needlecases, ornaments and a toothbrush. A few objects are decorative, but overall the collection emphasizes the ordinary items of daily life, and contains a significantly high proportion of artefacts to do with Inuit hunting, fishing, travel and survival methods, in which Rae took such a special interest.

After he left the Hudson's Bay Company in 1856 Rae continued to collect native artefacts whenever the opportunity arose. In 1860 he undertook the land part of a survey for a proposed telegraph line from England by way of the Faroe Islands, Iceland and Greenland to America, and while in Greenland he collected a number of Greenland Inuit items.

In 1864 Rae conducted another telegraph survey from Winnipeg across the Rocky Mountains to the Pacific coast, traversing some hundreds of miles of the most dangerous parts of the Fraser River in small dugout canoes without a guide. During this trip he added to his personal collection of Canadian ethnography over twenty Northwest Coast Indian artefacts including rattles, pipebowls, dishes and model canoes. Rae also seems to have taken an interest in Canadian Indian antiquities, because his personal collection includes such items as 'an instrument of bone, pointed like a tusk, belonging to Mada, hereditary medicine man to the Grand River Chippewas. Preserved in the family of Chief Johnston 100 years', and a knife blade described as 'the scalping knife of Mudjekeewis, Chief of the Kosheshebayaning branch of Ojibway Indians, 203 years old'.

Structures too large or otherwise unsuitable for collection, such as snowhouses and types of animal traps, were often recorded by Rae in sketches. He was a fluent draftsman, producing both finished drawings

Rae's notebook sketch of an Inuit snow-house.

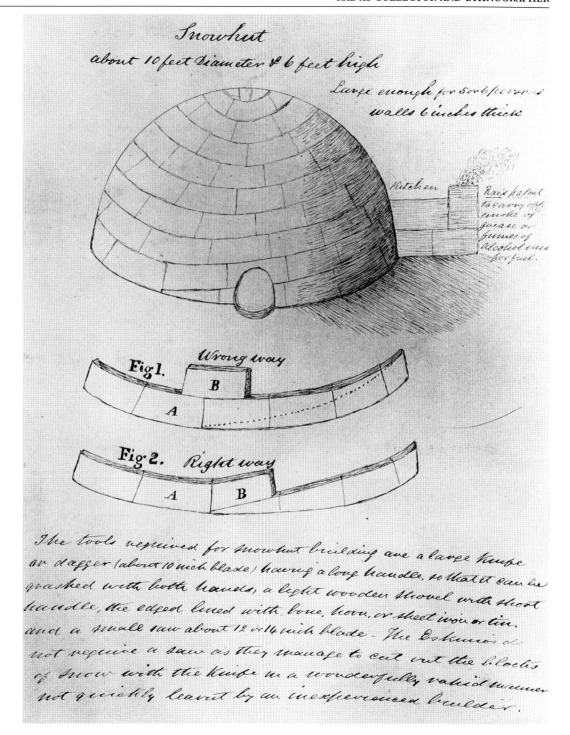

Snow hut

about 10 feet diameter & 6 feet high

Large enough for 5 or 6 persons

walls 6 inches thick

Kitchen

Rae's hat cut to carry off smoke of grease or fumes of alcohol used for fuel.

Fig 1.   Wrong way

B

A

Fig. 2.   Right way

A   B

The tools required for snow hut building are a large knife or dagger (about 10 inch blade) having a long handle, so that it can be grasped with both hands, a light wooden shovel with short handle, the edge lined with bone, horn, or sheet iron or tin, and a small saw about 12 or 14 inch blade.— The Eskimos do not require a saw as they manage to cut out the blocks of snow with the knife in a wonderfully rapid manner not quickly learnt by an inexperienced builder.

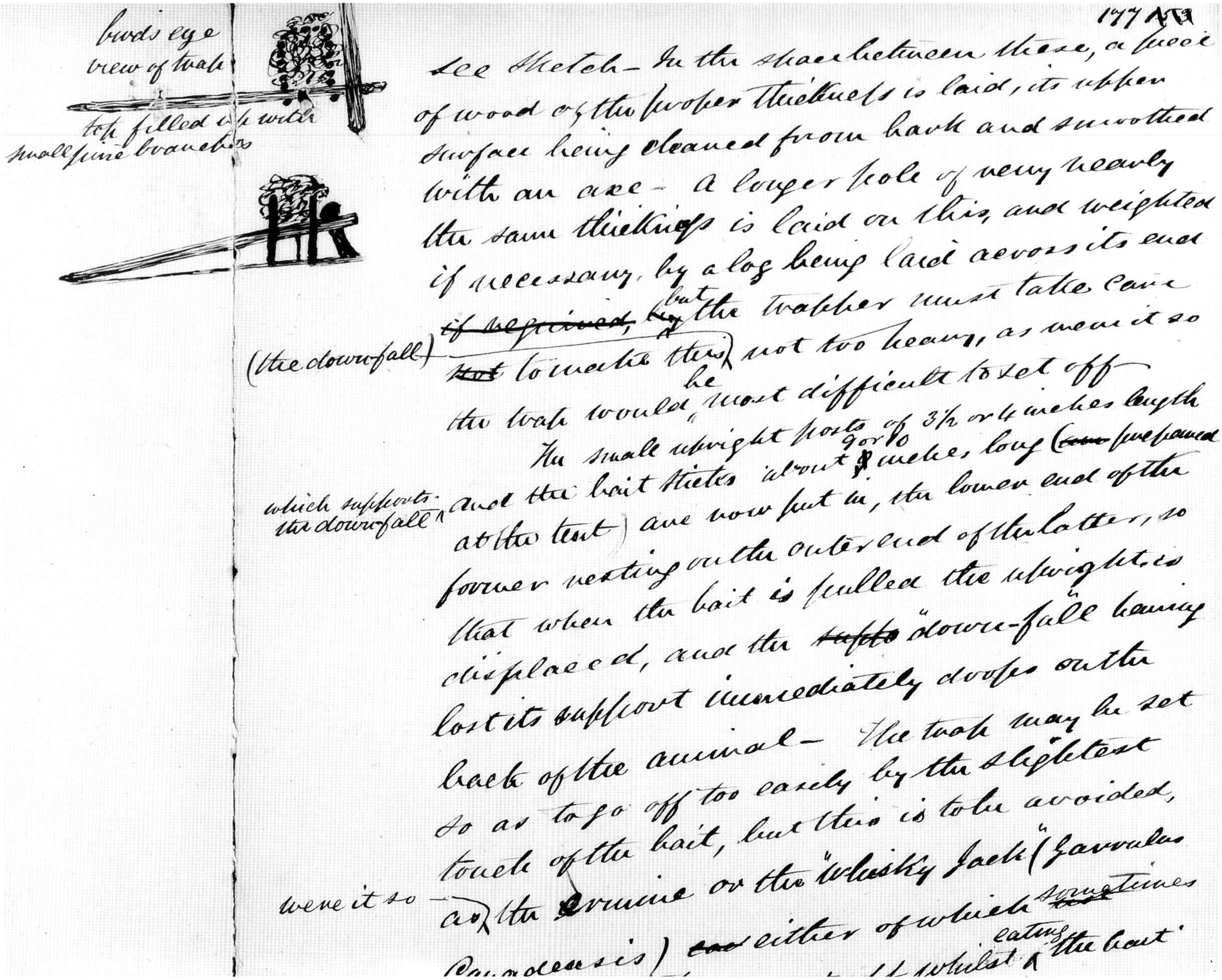

177

birds eye view of trap

top filled up with small pine branches

(the downfall)

which supports the downfall

were it so

Rae's sketch of an Indian animal trap, from his autobiography.

see sketch— In the space between these, a piece of wood of the proper thickness is laid, its upper surface being cleaned from bark and smoothed with an axe— A longer pole of very nearly the same thickness is laid on this, and weighted if necessary, by a log being laid across its end if required, but the trapper must take care to make this not too heavy, as were it so the trap would, be most difficult to set off. The small upright posts of 3½ or 4 inches length and the bait sticks about 9 or 10 inches long (are prepared at the tent) are now put in, its lower end of the former resting on the outer end of the latter, so that when the bait is pulled the uprights displaced, and the "down-fall" having lost its support immediately drops on the back of the animal— The trap may be set so as to go off too easily by the slightest touch of the bait, but this is to be avoided, as the Ermine or the "Whisky Jack" (Garrulus Pm. modeensis) either of which sometimes whilst eating the bait and roughly sketched impressions, although very few survive. Rae's appreciation of the skills needed to construct an Inuit snowhouse is evident in his annotated diagrammatic drawing. His enthusiasm for Inuit technology is shown in the rapid shorthand sketches he scribbled into the margins of his manuscript autobiography, perhaps as an aid in describing what he meant to his wife, Catherine, who sometimes wrote to his dictation.

In addition to his collection of artefacts, Rae's published and unpublished writings reveal a wealth of ethnographic detail and an admiration for aspects of native Canadian life. He describes Indian women, probably Cree, seen in the 1830s at Moose Factory, thus:

> The winter dresses of the women are made usually of stout blue cloth, cut rather short with leggings of the same, neatly ornamented with beads and ribbons, and they wear a curiously formed headdress of cloth, ornamented in the same manner as the leggings, which hangs down at the back so as to completely prevent the snow from getting between the neck and the dress, when walking through the woods or during a fall of snow.

In July 1846 at Repulse Bay he describes the Inuit women he meets:

> They were all tattooed on the face, hands and arms. Hair in a large bunch on each side of the head with a stick wrapped with deerskin in it. They all had ivory combs of their own manufacture, and deerskin clothes with the hair inwards. The only difference from the man's dress was the larger hood for the baby and the greater capacity of their boots which come above the knee and are attached to a girdle.

These comments are of interest although they do little more than confirm descriptions by earlier observers. Rae is at his best when analyzing Indian and Inuit technology in relation to survival techniques, particularly hunting and trapping, fishing, shelter and travel. For example, he describes in detail the way in which women trapped willow grouse in nets:

> The favourite feeding places of these white grouse are driftbanks of snow along the shores or river edge, high enough to cover up the willows, except their tops, so the birds can easily get at the buds - their favourite food - in some much frequented locality a net 4 or 5 yards square is placed being stretched on a light frame of wood, and propped up at one side by a stick 3

Indian with a trapped beaver. Detail from a drawing by T M Martin (1838-1934).

Inuit woman and child of Chesterfield Inlet, about 1930. *A E Porsild*

or 4 feet high, to which a long string is attached. A quantity of gravel is then strewed about on the snow under the net. To do this work well two people are required. The one, being usually a little boy or girl, concealed by a fence of brushwood or willows, who holds the long line attached to the prop ready to pull it when required, the other drives the pack birds in the desired direction, which necessitates some skill and much patience, as the driver has to keep the birds moving, but not to approach so near as to make them take flight. As soon as the birds get sight of the gravel they rush or fly to it, the line is pulled, the net dropped, and all or a great part are caught. Thirty or forty are thus sometimes taken at one haul.

The ecological advantages of native trapping methods over European ones were fully appreciated by Rae:

The beaver is very frequently caught in steel traps but there is another way in very common use which I had not seen described. When it has been decided to capture a family of beavers a number of wooden stakes are prepared at a short distance both above and below the house and simultaneously a trench is cut through the ice across the stream at these points, the stakes driven into the muddy bottom so close to each other that the beaver are unable to get through. A net being then set round the house its walls are broken down and the beavers get entangled in the net. The advantage of this plan is that the trapper has the option of letting go those which owing to size or other reasons is not desirable to retain, which cannot be done when traps are used, the animals are either then dead or too much injured to live.

Rae was constantly fascinated by the bird and animal behaviour that he observed. He described how, while hunting hares on Wollaston Peninsula in 1851:

I noticed one animal that looked different from the others ... This proved to be a white fox that had tucked his long bushy tail underneath, hopped about, and sat up occasionally exactly as his companions did, always edging nearer and nearer to them.

He was impressed by the ways in which native Canadian hunters took advantage of their knowledge of animal behaviour:

The Indian, who has thoroughly studied the habits of the bird (blue winged goose) takes advantage of her affection for her young, and of their attachment to their parent, to make both his prey ... knowing that the young are

Beaver - crucial to the early opening up of Canada. *W Lynch*

Arctic fox and hare - Rae's description emphasizes their similarity. (Left, *W Lynch* right, *I K MacNeil*)

Willow grouse in winter and spring plumage. (Left, *Fred Bruemmer* right, *W Lynch*)

Musk ox formed into a circle for defense, Ellesmere Island, and musk ox in close-up. *M Beedell*

Opposite: Female polar bear with young, Ellesmere Island. *W Lynch*

easily decoyed by imitating their call and by mock geese set up in the marsh, and that the old bird, although more shy, will follow them, he waits patiently until she comes within range; if he shoots her, he is pretty sure to kill the greater part of the others, as they continue to fly over and around the place for some time after.

Rae was keen to acquire zoological specimens for museums in England. His attempts to collect bear and musk ox skeletons were not always successful, 'because the Indians have a superstition about it being unlucky to preserve the bones, or at least all of them, of any single animal'. But in 1853 he listed five complete musk ox skeletons and skins prepared from animals shot at Repulse Bay, which, together with several specimens of Arctic birds, are now in the collection of the Natural History Museum, London. Rae also retained in his own possession the trophy heads of six deer and caribou which are today mounted in the entrance hall of the Department of Anatomy in the University of Edinburgh.

The evident interest that Rae took in the artefacts in his collection is unusual for the period. Many are labelled in his own hand with

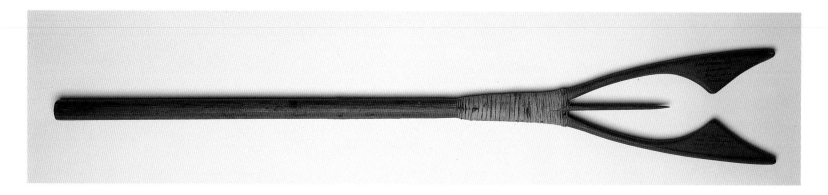

Replica Micmac Indians fishing spear made by Rae, and, in close-up, the same spear showing Rae's own notes.

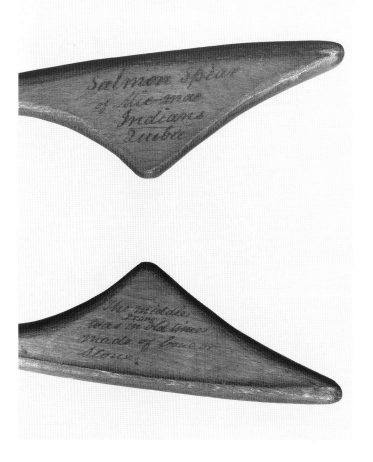

descriptions of their manufacture and use. Well ahead of his time in his practical understanding of aspects of native Canadian technology, Rae tried hard to convince his contemporaries of their scientific value, through demonstrations, lectures and publications.

On retiring from the Hudson's Bay Company in 1856 he made his base in London, giving lectures and writing articles for various learned societies, including the Royal Geographical Society. In 1882 at a lecture to the Society of Arts he argued, 'I may be laughed at for saying that the Eskimo are scientific; but I think I can prove the fact', and went on to analyze the specific qualities of snowgoggles, snowhouses, iced sledge runners, kayaks, salmon spears and harpoons, and the correct treatment for frostbite. 'Demonstrations' of artefacts at meetings were common among antiquarian and other scientific organizations at this period. Rae was able to draw upon his own collection of artefacts for lecture aids, such as the Inuit stone lamp and the Repulse Bay fish spear. The latter he described in 1877 at a lecture at the Royal Institution, as 'far superior in almost every respect to anything of the kind I have ever seen used by civilized man'. He even made as a demonstration piece a replica of a Micmac fishing spearhead, which he inscribed as follows: 'Model made by John Rae, 2 Addison Gardens, London. The handle should be 7 or 8 feet long. Salmon spear of Micmac Indians of Quebec. Middle prong was in old times made of bone or stone. To spear fish of 6 to 30 or 40 lbs weight. The long outer prongs are usually made of birch or other tough elastic wood which becomes pliant when wet', adding in a further note: 'the wood of the model is too stout and heavy with not sufficient elasticity'.

Rae was in practice what today we would call an ethnographer, a student of Canadian ethnology or material culture, and his collections and written accounts are now recognized as valuable evidence of unique lifeways which have undergone considerable change since the period of initial European contact. A century after Rae's death, the native peoples of the Canadian north have adapted to the modern world, yet many continue to practise the hunting and trapping skills which Rae so admired and emulated.

SOME LEADING FIGURES OF
ARCTIC EXPLORATION
1817-60

Sir George Back 1796-1878
Member of Franklin expeditions of 1819 and 1824. Led expeditions in 1833 and 1836 with HMS *Terror* to trace the coast between Repulse Bay and Point Turnagain. Artist. Spent eight winters in the Arctic. Later, became vice-president of the Royal Geographical Society.

Sir John Barrow 1764-1848
Second Secretary at the Admiralty from 1804 for about 40 years. Determined encourager of the search for the north-west passage. Planned first nineteenth-century Arctic expeditions, especially Ross expedition of 1818.

Frederick Beechey 1796-1856
First officer on the *Trent*, John Ross expedition 1818, and with Parry in 1819. Captain of the *Blossom*, which sailed from the Pacific to rendezvous with Franklin's 1824 expedition. Reached Point Barrow 1825. Became President of the Royal Geographical Society 1855.

Sir Edward Belcher 1799-1877
Sailed with Beechey in 1825. Led 1850 Franklin search expedition with HMS *Assistance*, HMS *Resolute*, HMS *Intrepid*, HMS *Pioneer*, and HMS *North Star*. Criticized for too readily abandoning his ships when ice-bound.

William Corrigal
From Orphir, Orkney, joined Hudson's Bay Company in 1837, one of the large numbers of Orcadians employed by them. Accompanied Rae's 1846-7 expedition as a steersman, and was highly thought of by Rae. Left the Company in 1848 to live in the Red River Settlement.

Peter Warren Dease
Chief Factor with the Hudson's Bay Company. Member of the second Franklin expedition, 1825. With Thomas Simpson explored west to Point Barrow and east to the mouth of Castor and Pollux River, 1837-8.

Sir John Franklin 1786-1847
Commanded the overland expedition of 1819 to chart the north coast of America and expedition of 1824 (with Richardson) to survey the coast west of the Mackenzie River. Commander of 1845 expedition, with *Erebus* and *Terror*, on which he went missing.

Lady Franklin 1792-1875
Jane Griffin, Franklin's second wife (married 1828). Initiated search for Franklin in 1847, and continued efforts for 13 years. Sponsored four Arctic expeditions, offering a reward of £2000 for information. Fitted out the *Pandora* in 1875 for another attempt at the north-west passage.

Robert Hood
Midshipman on Franklin expedition of 1819. Artist. Shot, possibly by the *voyageur* Michel, in 1821. Michel claimed a gun had gone off accidentally.

Dr Richard King 1818-79
Surgeon, naturalist and ethnologist, second-in-command of Back's 1833 Franklin search expedition. Had strong and vociferously expressed views as to the strategy for later search expeditions, but regarded as eccentric. Assistant surgeon on the *Resolute*, 1850 search expedition.

Sir Robert McClure 1807-73
Mate with Back on the *Terror*, 1836, and 1st lieutenant with J M Ross on the *Investigator*. Captain of the *Investigator* in one of the 1850 Franklin search expeditions, entering the Arctic from the Pacific. Completed the north-west passage from west to east, 1853.

Thomas Mistegan
Cree Indian, 'of great intelligence and activity' (Rae), excellent shot, skilled hunter and sledge hauler. Accompanied Rae's fourth expedition, 1853, and several later expeditions.

Albert One-Eye
Inuit interpreter and boatman to Sir John Richardson's 1848 expedition. Accompanied Rae when the expedition split into two groups, and was drowned while travelling on the Coppermine River.

Ouligbuck
Experienced Inuit hunter, boatman and interpreter who participated in several expeditions, including Franklin 1825-7, Dease and Simpson 1836 and Rae 1846-7.

William Ouligbuck
Son of Ouligbuck, also a hunter and interpreter and accompanied Franklin 1825-7, Rae 1846-7 and 1853. Less reliable than his father, but a good interpreter - reputedly spoke ten languages.

Sir William Edward Parry 1790-1855
Captain of the *Alexander* on John Ross's 1818 expedition and commander of the 1819 expedition, with *Hecla* and *Griper*. Commanded the third Arctic expedition, of 1821, with *Hecla* and *Fury*, and a fourth of 1824, again with *Hecla* and *Fury*. Became rear-admiral in 1852.

Sir John Richardson 1787-1865
Surgeon and naturalist. Member of Franklin expeditions of 1819-22 and 1825-7. Led 1848 overland Franklin search expedition down the Mackenzie River, accompanied by John Rae. Collected natural history material now in UK museums and made important contributions to ichthyology studies.

George Rivers
Cree Indian, skilled hunter, trapper and mentor to John Rae when he was based at Moose Factory. His teaching helped to equip Rae for the rigours of his later travels.

Sir James Clark Ross 1800-62
Nephew of John Ross, and accompanied him on the 1818 expedition. A member of John Ross's 1829 expedition and located the Magnetic Pole in 1831. Commanded the *Cove* in 1836 relief expedition to trapped whalers. Commanded one of the 1848 Franklin search expeditions, with HMS *Enterprise* and HMS *Investigator*. Also travelled in the Antarctic.

Sir John Ross 1777-1856
Commander of the first expedition to the Arctic after the Napoleonic Wars, with *Isabella, Alexander, Trent,* and *Dorothea*. Commanded the 1829 expedition with steam packet *Victory*, backed by HBC and Felix Booth of Booth's Gin. Led 1850 Franklin search expedition with the *Felix*.

William Scoresby 1789-1857
English whaling captain based in Whitby, whose 1817 report on melting pack ice encouraged a renewed effort to seek the north-west passage. Associate of Professor Robert Jameson and Sir Joseph Banks, who both benefited from his Arctic knowledge.

Sir George Simpson 1792-1860
Scottish born, joined HBC in 1820, became Governor of Northern Department 1821. Travelled extensively in Canada, traversing the continent in 1828, the year he became Overseas Governor of the Company. Played a key role in enabling and encouraging Rae in particular and Arctic exploration in general.

CHRONOLOGY

JOHN RAE
AND ARCTIC EXPLORATION

1813 John Rae born 30 September at Hall of Clestrain, Orkney

1817 Scoresby reports on conditions in the Arctic

1818 John Ross expedition (*Isabella* and *Alexander*)

1819 Parry expedition (*Hecla* and *Griper*)

1821 Hudson's Bay Company merges with North West Company

Parry expedition (*Hecla* and *Fury*)

1824 Parry expedition (*Fury*)

1825 Franklin expedition

1828 George Simpson becomes Governor in Chief of Hudson's Bay Company territories

1829 John & James Clark Ross expedition (*Victory*)

Rae attends Edinburgh University

1831 James Clark Ross locates Magnetic Pole

1833 Rae qualifies as surgeon and joins HBC supply ship *Prince of Wales*

Back expedition

1834 Rae accepts post as surgeon at HBC's Moose Factory

1836 James Clark Ross expedition (*Cove*)

1837 Thomas Simpson and Peter Warren Dease overland expedition

Back expedition (*Terror*)

1845 Franklin expedition

Rae receives training in surveying in Toronto

1846-7 Rae's first expedition: to Repulse Bay, maps shores of Committee Bay

1847 Rae in England

1848-9 Rae's second expedition, with Sir John Richardson, one of three Franklin search expeditions: from mouth of the Mackenzie River east to the Coppermine River, with attempt by Rae to reach Wollaston Peninsula

1849 Rae takes up post as Chief Factor at Fort Simpson

1850 Franklin search expeditions led by Sir John Ross: *Felix* Collinson and McClure expedition: *Enterprise* and *Investigator*

1850-1 Rae's third expedition, in search of Franklin: from Great Bear Lake down Coppermine, maps southern shore Victoria Island and Wollaston Peninsula, travels an average of over 27 miles a day

1852 Rae in England

1853-4 Rae's last Arctic expedition: to Repulse Bay to complete survey of west shore of Boothia, discovers Rae Strait between Boothia and King William Island thus establishing existence of north-west passage

1854 McClure completes west-east negotiation of north-west passage

Rae discovers first evidence of fate of Franklin expedition

Rae in England

1856 Rae and his party receive British Government award for Rae's discovery of Franklin evidence, of which £8000 goes to Rae

1857 Franklin search expedition led by Captain McClintock: *Fox*

1857-9 Rae lives in Hamilton, Ontario

1860 Rae marries Catherine Jane Alicia (Kate) Thompson in Toronto and returns with her to Britain

1864 Rae conducts survey across Greenland for the Atlantic Telegraph Company

1865-7 Rae at Berstane House, Orkney

1867 Rae returns to London and continues to take an active interest in all matters concerned with the Arctic and Canada

1893 Dies in London on 22 July, buried in Kirkwall, Orkney

CONTRIBUTORS

Ian Bunyan, Education Officer, National Museums of Scotland, author of *R34: Twice Across the Atlantic* (NMS) and *Polar Scots: Scottish Explorers in the Arctic and Antarctic* (NMS). Has studied Arctic exploration through an interest in Arctic material in the NMS collections.

Jenni Calder, Head of Publications, National Museums of Scotland, author of numerous books and articles including *RLS: A Life Study* (Hamish Hamilton), *Scotland in Trust* (Drew) and 'Perilous Enterprise: Scottish Explorers in the Arctic' in *The Enterprising Scot* (HMSO).

Dale Idiens, Depute Director (Collections), Keeper, Department of History and Applied Art, National Museums of Scotland, ethnographer and author of articles and catalogues on North American Indians and Inuit - the NMS has one of the most important collections of Inuit material in the UK. Curator of the exhibition 'No Ordinary Journey: John Rae, Arctic Explorer'.

Bryce Wilson, native of Stromness, Orkney, and since 1972 Museums Officer with Orkney Islands Council with a particular interest in Orkney's Hudson's Bay Company links. Author of *The Lighthouses of Orkney* (Stromness Museum) and *Sea Haven: Stromness in the Orkney Islands* (The Orkney Press).

ACKNOWLEDGEMENTS

This book would not have been possible without the picture research and advice and guidance provided by Elizabeth Robertson, NMS. We wish also to thank Brian Donat and Ann Newton for help with picture research in Canada, and the Scott Polar Research Institute, Cambridge, for providing a copy of John Rae's unpublished autobiography.

Maps drawn by Stephen Gibson.

Illustration credits:

By permission of the British Library 89

Collection of Glenbow Museum, Calgary, Alberta Frontispiece 55.17.1

Dartmouth College Library 103

Environment Canada/Parks Service 31, 51, 55, 57, 72, 106, 107 above and below right, 108, 109

Hudson's Bay Company Archives, Provincial Archives of Manitoba 47, 48, 56, 59

National Archives of Canada, v (C-27815), x (C-93106), xi (C-133769), 15 (C-100067), 19 (C-38856), 21 (C-1918), 22 above (C-40327), below (C-114508), 23 (C-40360), 24 right (C-28847), 25 (C-94128), 26 (C-93021), 27 left (C-93042), right (C-93036), 28 (C-94145), 29 (C-93315), 30 (C-94148), 35 (C-229), 37 (C-6699), 41 (C-20610), 42 (C-133785), 44 (C-94141), 46 (C-40321), 50 above (PA183369), below (PA-182561), 60 (C-27815), 61 (C-27831), 62 right (C-133829), centre (C-133832), 64 left (PA-147990), 66 (C-1917), 69 right (C-1060), 71 (C-38951), 74 (C-93039), 75 (C-102852), 79 above (C-40198), 81 above left (PA-73910), below (C-38174), 85 (C-133775), 87 above (C-15257), below (C-28848), 88 (C-97301), 94 above (C-93027), 105 above (C-90370), below (PA-101006)

Trustees of the National Library of Scotland 3, 12, 17

Trustees of the National Museums of Scotland viii, 8 below, 16, 36, 40, 62 left, 64 right, 78, 79 below, 81 right, 82, 84, 92, 94 below, 95, 98, 100, 101, 102, 110

By courtesy of the National Portrait Gallery, London 33, 39, 54

By courtesy of the Orkney Library - Photographic Archive 8 above left and right, 10, 63, 69 left

Pier Arts Centre 9

Scott Polar Research Institute 104

Scottish National Portrait Gallery 97